Bailout

Bailout

*What the Rescue of Bear
Stearns and the Credit
Crisis Mean for Your
Investments*

John M. Waggoner

WILEY

John Wiley & Sons, Inc.

Published by John Wiley & Sons, Inc., Hoboken, New Jersey.
Published simultaneously in Canada.

For general information on our other products and services or for technical support, please contact our Customer Care Department within the United States at (800) 762-2974, outside the United States at (317) 572-3993 or fax (317) 572-4002.

Wiley also publishes its books in a variety of electronic formats. Some content that appears in print may not be available in electronic books. For more information about Wiley products, visit our web site at www.wiley.com.

Library of Congress Cataloging-in-Publication Data

Waggoner, John M.
    Bailout : what the rescue of Bear Stearns and the credit crisis mean for your investments / John M. Waggoner.
        p.   cm.
    Includes bibliographical references and index.
    ISBN 978-0-470-40125-5 (cloth)
        1. Investments.   2. Financial crises.   I. Title.
    HG4521.W155 2008
    332.6—dc22

                                                                    2008032175

Printed in the United States of America

10 9 8 7 6 5 4 3 2 1

In memory of my parents, Miles Waggoner and Dorothy Mundinger, and with love for my children, Nate and Hope Waggoner

Contents

Acknowledgments

First, I'd like to thank Debra Englander, my editor, and Kelly O'Connor, Wiley's development editor, for their support and great patience.

When you work in a newsroom, anything you do is often the result of your interactions with your fellow reporters and editors. Sandra Block, Christine Dugas, and Cathy Chu are friends of the best kind: They can tell you when your ideas are good and when they're bad, and in either case, you still wind up laughing about it. I can always talk about the markets with David Craig, Matt Krantz, and Adam Shell, and I always come away with help and encouragement. Nancy Blair, Fred Monyak, and Tom Fogarty can make me look much better than I am and they do it with grace. The folks who run the Money section—Jim Henderson, Geri Tucker, and Rodney Brooks—are one reason it's so consistently good. And Mary Ann Cristiano's love, encouragement, and patience helped me more than I can possibly say.

Bailout

Chapter 1

What Just Happened Here?

If you have ever woken up in the lemur cage at the zoo—and who hasn't?—you know that most true disasters start innocently enough. In this case, it all started with a night out with your buddies. You drank. You talked. You ordered a martini. It tasted good.

Pretty soon, someone suggested moving to Snickenfelder's, where they have a list of martinis longer than the menu. Good idea! After all, Snickenfelder's was just down the street. And when you got there, you were confronted with more alcoholic concoctions than you thought possible. You tried an apricot mango martini. Yum. An orange chocolate martini. Wow. On reflection, your mistake was ordering the Snickenfelder Schnocker, made with vodka, hazelnut liquor, amaretto, Irish cream, Kahlua, and more vodka.

You vaguely recall the karaoke contest, but you have to admit that you probably did not understand the rules when you got up on the stage. "Unbroken Melody" was probably a bad choice, given your state. At any rate, here you are, covered in peanut butter and surrounded by cooing primates.

In March of 2008, the world markets woke up with one of the ugliest hangovers in history. Bear Stearns, the fifth-largest U.S. investment bank found itself in the financial equivalent of the drunk tank: Sequestered with federal regulators and pitiless bidders for the remnants of its assets.

It was a nasty, nasty, bender that put Bear Stearns in the lockup, the sort of sudden decline that smacks of Victorian morality tales. Just two years earlier, Bear Stearns was a titan of finance, happily ensconced at its massive $1.3 billion head-quarters at 383 Madison Avenue in New York. It had thousands of employees working around the globe, billions of dollars in assets, and a varied business in stocks, bonds, derivatives, and financial counseling for the very rich.

In short, Bear Stearns was a very big, very important company, one with tremendous earnings and global clout. And Bear Stearns remained a very big, very important company right up until the second week of March, 2008. On March 7, 2008, the company's stock closed at $70.08—well off its 2007 highs, but nearly every financial stock had been clobbered in 2008.

The next trading day, Monday, March 10, the stock slid more than 10 percent and closed at $62.30. Tuesday, it fell to $55. After a slight rally on the 12th, it slipped below $60 again. Then, on Friday, the stock collapsed, plunging to $30 a share. But the worst was yet to come.

Late on Sunday, March 16, word came out that arch rival JPMorgan Chase had bid just $2 a share for Bear Stearns, and the company had accepted it. By the end of trading on March 17, 2008, Bear Stock was trading at $4.81 a share. The $2 price tag was just too low for Wall Street to believe—and rightly so, as it turned out.

"*JP Morgan Bags Wounded Bear—Bargain-basement $235 million for Reeling Giant*," read the March 17 headline of the *New York Post*.[1] JPMorgan Chase bought all of Bear Stearns for about a fifth of the value of its Manhattan headquarters alone. Later that week, bowing to threats of lawsuits, JPMorgan Chase upped the Bear bid to $10 a share—still, on its face, a tremendous bargain.

By the end of the Bear Stearns saga, there were plenty of ruined investors. Employees who had kept money in Bear Stearns stock were essentially wiped out. (Top management, who had many more shares, fared far better than the rank and file). But big companies fail all the time and, to be honest, they leave little mark of their passage, except for the holes they leave in the lives (and retirement accounts) of their workers.

When Bear Stearns collapsed, however, it nearly crippled the short-term money market, the lifeblood of modern finance. Bank lending ground to a halt. Municipal financing, which pays for roads, schools, and other daily essentials, evaporated. The company's fall changed the way the government regulates Wall Street, and it shook the faith of investors to the core—and justifiably so.

The Herd on the Street

How did it happen?

Periods of intoxication generally begin with sobriety, and it is the nature of manias that they start out perfectly sane. So we are going to detail, in the next chapter, the relatively sober beginnings of the bubble that eventually bagged Bear. As you will see, things made a great deal of sense.

From 2005 until August, 2007 was the period of pure mania. Most of us are familiar with the boom in housing, but it is still interesting to recap, if only for sheer, eye-popping detail and *shadenfreude*. We will visit a small, somewhat representative town in suburban Washington to illustrate what soaring house prices can do to otherwise sober citizens.

But the real bubble—the one that took down Bear Stearns—wasn't in the real estate market. It was in the debt market. We think of bonds as a kind of investment for Old Money, the folks who would visit the bank vault every few months, clip a few coupons, and redeem them for walking-around money.

In fact, the bond bulls had run on Wall Street for a very, very long time. The bull market in stocks ran from August 1982 and ended (according to some views) in March, 2002, propelling the Dow up about 1,200 percent. (See Figure 1.1.)

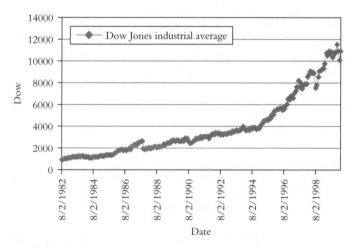

Figure 1.1   The Super Bull Market in Stocks, 1982–2000

But the bull market in bonds ran far longer. We will explain this in detail in Chapter 3, but bonds prices rise when interest rates fall. The yield on the bellwether 10-year Treasury bond fell from a high of 15.83 percent in September 1981 to a low of 3.35 percent in May 2003. For the past 10 years, you would have made far more money investing in bonds than you would have investing in stocks. (See Figure 1.2.)

We haven't seen a bear market for bonds in many, many years—and what brought down Bear Stearns was not the stock market, but the bond market. Bear Stearns nearly went bankrupt because the bonds it packaged and sold to investors were so incredibly bad. Eventually, Bears' creditors suspected that the company's assets were virtually worthless—and lending to a company with worthless assets is simply throwing good money after bad. At the very end, when Bear Stearns could not even get short-term lending, the company was forced to a

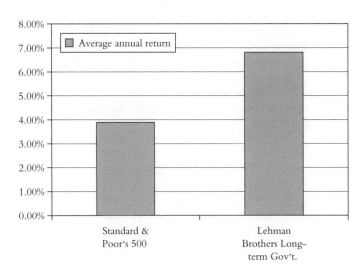

Figure 1.2 Stocks vs. Bonds, 10 years

great reckoning in a small room—the sale of itself for the fire-sale price of $2 a share to JPMorgan Chase.

Bear Lessons

The question, then, becomes what does the bear market in bonds and the demise of Bear Stearns mean for your investments? We can start with a few calming observations: For one thing, the system worked. We are not in a worldwide depression, the banking system is still functioning, and people get up and go to work every morning. The Federal Reserve did its job, and with some alacrity, too. All that's for the good.

Once that is settled, though, we have to ask a few questions about how we save and invest. We must, of course, assume that somehow the world will muddle through. Otherwise, we may as well hunker down in a bunker, eating canned food, and cradling our rifles.

For that reason, your core plan for investing—using a mixture of stocks, bonds, and money market securities to meet your goals—should not be radically different. We're not going to suggest you throw out decades of financial research and put all your money into gold or plastics or Irish punts. And in Chapter 5, we will give you some guidance on how to set up your basic plan of attack.

That said, we should also note that the world economic system is increasingly complex and precarious. For example, the use of derivatives among financial institutions is soaring. These are legal contracts between two parties: Their value is derived from the movements in various market indices, which is where the word "derivatives" come from. Currently, there are about $55 trillion in derivatives outstanding, which is roughly five times the value of all the goods and services produced in the United States each year.

Warren Buffett, CEO of Berkshire Hathaway and the world's wealthiest man, knows a thing or two about risk. He had this to say about derivatives in 2007:

> I believe we may not know where exactly the danger begins and at what point it becomes a super danger. We don't know when it will end precisely, but . . . at some point some very unpleasant things will happen in markets.[2]

As investors, we have other worries, too. The U.S. debt now totals $9 trillion, close to a record in relation to our gross domestic product. The Treasury's credit rating is the world's gold standard. In times of crisis, in fact, people buy Treasuries, not gold, even though gold has been the world's fallback currency since Nebuchadnezzar was in short pants.

Unfortunately, we are not working earnestly to repay those debts. We're adding merrily to them, to the tune of $2 billion a day. A billion here and a billion there, as Senator Everett Dirksen once said, and pretty soon you're talking real money.

Even worse, the U.S. doesn't save enough of it to count on the public to buy them. It has to rely on other governments to buy our daily $2 billion of Treasury securities. So far, that has worked just fine—although it has put a great deal of pressure on the U.S. dollar. Should other countries say one day, "Thanks, we just need $1.5 billion today," then the dollar could quickly fall from the gold standard to the silver standard. (See Figure 1.3).

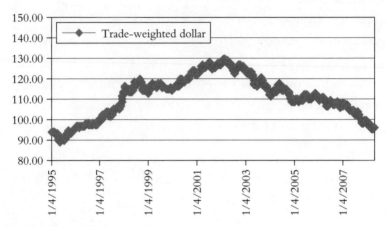

Figure 1.3 Trade-Weighted Dollar Index

Investors, then, need to take a few precautions against catastrophe. One potential catastrophe is debt liquidation—the type we came perilously close to seeing when Bear Stearns collapsed. Debt liquidation simply means cascading defaults, which will ultimately lead to a Depression-like economic downturn. There are some schools of thought that this kind of event—which occurred with depressing frequency in the 19th century—is actually good for the economy, a kind of economic cleansing process. These are the same kind of people who giggle during horror movies, too.

In Chapter 6, we will start with the most basic way to protect yourself from deflation: Paying down your debt. You may recall your grandmother warning you about the peril of debt. And you know what? She was right. It makes no sense to plan a portfolio that returns 12 percent when you are paying 25 percent to your credit card company.

Once again, let's not get carried away: Some debt is good. If you have a 6 percent mortgage and can afford the payments, then relax. That is cheap money—and you can probably earn better returns elsewhere than what you would get from paying down your mortgage early.

Your portfolio, too, can be clobbered by deflation. Although some stocks might weather deflation well—nasty businesses like payday lending companies come to mind—you might be better off by adding some high-quality bonds to your portfolio. Think of it this way: If you get $100 a month from your bonds each month and prices fall, your bond becomes increasingly lovely in the eyes of other investors—and they will pay you a premium for it.

Another solution to our massive debt problem isn't much more palatable. If the government allows higher inflation, it can repay its debt with progressively cheaper money. But that means that the price of food, gas, and other essential rises too—which ultimately impoverishes everyone. Inflation has been called the cruelest tax, because it hurts those on a fixed income most—like people who live on pensions or periodic withdrawals from their savings.

Not too long ago, there was one hedge against inflation: gold. And it's still an inflation hedge, albeit one that's annoying to store and pays no dividends. But today you have several other options for fighting inflation, such as Treasury Inflation-Protected Securities, or TIPS. We will run through your inflation-fighting options in Chapter 7.

Finally, we must remember that booms and busts are part of the fabric of capitalist society. And it is fabulously easy to get caught up in the boom, and crunched in the bust. How can you tell if Wall Street has left the world of the rational and gone straight to the laughable? It is not easy, but there are signs, and good ones. We will talk about those in Chapter 8.

Kurt Vonnegut, author of *Slaughterhouse Five,* among other novels, once said that the only thing we can learn from history is to be surprised. He's quite right. Somewhere along the way, the people at Bear Stearns—and much of the rest of Wall Street—felt that there was nothing to be surprised about.

As an investor, you can make intelligent guesses about what the future will be like. But there will always be surprises. For that reason, you need to cast your net far and wide to protect—as best you can—against the unexpected. There will be days when your small insurance positions in foreign bonds or commodity funds will make you feel like the village idiot. That's ok. When you invest, making gains are just part of the game. The other part is keeping them. It is a lesson that Bear Stearns could have learned a little better.

Chapter 2

How Did It All Begin?

We like to think of the men and women on Wall Street as serious-minded, sober people. In fact, Wall Streeters cultivate this image. Nearly every ad for a brokerage house, mutual fund, or investment bank features a conservatively dressed man or woman in a wood-paneled room, arms crossed, glasses in hand, looking thoughtfully into the distance. (By law, they can't show pictures of people rolling around in piles of money.)

Now, people who occupy the world of finance are, by and large, exceptionally smart people. They typically come from Ivy League colleges, sport advanced degrees, and have very nice taste in clothing. They take their work quite seriously.

Nevertheless, from time to time, people in the financial world go quite mad, no matter what their IQs. It's a phenomenon that has been observed for centuries.

In his classic 1857 work, *Memoirs of Extraordinary Popular Delusions and the Madness of Crowds*, Charles MacKay noted, "Sober nations have all at once become desperate gamblers, and risked almost their existence upon the turn of a piece of paper . . . Men, it has been well said, think in herds; it will be seen that they go mad in herds, while they only recover their senses slowly, and one by one."

Manias, like that first drink at the bar, almost always start soberly. The South Seas Bubble, for example, was founded on the entirely rational notion that Latin America, in the early 18th century, had a vast store of natural resources that could be incredibly lucrative for a company to exploit, particularly if the company had the backing of the English government.

Investors simply got *too* carried away with that notion. Suddenly, no price was too high to pay for stock in the South Seas Company, or the many other new corporations formed during the South Seas madness. (One company raised money for a venture so profitable it couldn't tell its investors what it was.)

The price of one share of the South Seas Company went from £100 to £1,000 in the course of 18 months. (For the curious, £1,000 in 1720 is worth £132,743 today,[1] or, at current exchange rates, about $261,500. Isaac Newton, who was no dummy, lost a small fortune in the South Seas Company. When the bubble burst, Newton reportedly lamented, "I can calculate the motions of heavenly bodies, but not the madness of people."

Similarly, to use a more recent example, it was entirely logical to think in, say, 1996, that the Internet was a pretty darn big thing and that it might have fascinating commercial potential. Why, you could order books online! And type messages to friends! And, perhaps, someday, even watch movies!

Technology stocks were also buoyed by the rather mad assumption that the Entire World as We Know It would be demolished by a computer glitch called the Y2K problem. In a nutshell, the Y2K problem was this: Back in the old days—the 1980s—computer memory was hard to come by. To save a bit or two, programmers used two digits rather than four. As the clock turned from 1999 to 2000, people feared that all computers would go haywire—not only messing up bank records and Social Security payouts, but electrical stations and nuclear power plants, too.

Many companies, rather than fix all their software bit by bit, simply bought new equipment that was Y2K compliant. You can only imagine the glee in an IT person's eyes when handed a huge budget and told to replace everything in the building. All that wild spending went straight to the earnings of all manner of technology companies, from consultants to software and hardware manufacturers.

But investors simply took a reasonable assumption—that technology had good growth potential—and blew it all out of financial proportion. Yes, the Internet was capable of many wonderful things, but not in 1996. People paid too much for corporate earnings that were too far in the future—or for earnings that never materialized, which is one of the problems with technology in general. They get carried away.

The technology-laden NASDAQ stock index rocketed 110 percent in the 12 months that ended March 10, 2000. Some technology stocks sold for several hundred times their past 12 months' earnings. Other Internet companies soared with little else but a CEO, three computers, and a name that ended in .com.

The bubble that took down Bear Stearns had three ingredients: houses, mortgages, and mortgaged-backed securities. All three, separately, aren't usually considered a bubble cocktail. Stir them all together? Ummmm. Bubbly.

Bust to Boom Again

Manias, at least the financial types, are generally rare, occurring perhaps once a generation. But the mania that engulfed Bear Stearns had its roots, ironically enough, in the popping of the technology bubble of the 1990s.

By 2000, the tech boom had gone to bust. The tech-laden NASDAQ stock index deflated at a rate rarely seen for a broad-based market index. One year after its March 10, 2000 peak, the NASDAQ was down 62 percent—one of the worst bear markets in living memory. Even now, more than seven years later, the Nazz is still down nearly 50 percent from its 2000 highs.

But the NASDAQ—and stock prices generally—were not the only things deflating. The market for new stock issues, or initial public offerings, dried up entirely. Lenders no longer showered companies with millions of dollars for technological expansion.

And many of those people who worked for startup companies like Pets.com were suddenly out of work. Although no one knew it at the time, a recession had started in July 2000 and ended in March 2001. (The National Bureau of Economic Research's Business Cycle Dating Committee, which works with great deliberation, did not declare the beginning of the recession until March 2001, the date when the committee later decided the recession had ended.) Unemployment, which was 3.8 percent in April 2000, nearly doubled to 6.3 percent by May 2003.

As unemployment crept up, prices slid down. By 2003, the producer price index, which measures inflation at the wholesale level, was trending downward. Cheap goods from China and elsewhere were pushing prices down. Suddenly, Wall Street—and, most importantly, the Federal Reserve—was worried about deflation.

The fed Chairman Alan Greenspan said as much in Congressional testimony in May 2003: Deflation "is a very serious issue and an issue to which we at the Federal Reserve are paying extensive attention." Greenspan went on to say, "Even though we perceive the risks as minor, the potential consequences are very substantial and could be quite negative."[2]

The worst outbreak of deflation in recent memory was, of course, the Great Depression. The specter of the Great Depression must haunt every Fed chairman's mind. Who wants to be known as the Fed chairman who led the country into another Great Depression?

The Depression was a deflationary spiral. As the economy slowed, people lost their jobs. Prices fell because no one had money to buy things. You could cut prices all you wanted, and your inventory would still languish. As spending slowed, so did employment, creating a vicious cycle that would lead to the worst economic period in 20th-century history.

The situation in 2002 and 2003 wasn't as dire as the Depression, but it was certainly worrisome. What truly terrified the Fed was the prospect of a Japanese-style deflationary slowdown. Japan's deflationary recession ground on for more than a decade.

And, at least at first blush, Japan's problems seemed a lot like our own. The Japanese deflation began when its stock-market bubble burst in 1989. (Their real estate bubble popped at the same time.) Their banking system was in shambles, primarily because of bad real estate loans. And waves of cheap Chinese imports kept prices falling.

Alan Greenspan summed up his worries about the U.S. economy in May 2003, during his testimony to Congress:

> Once again this year, our economy has struggled to surmount new obstacles. As the tensions with Iraq increased early in 2003, uncertainties surrounding a possible war contributed to a softening in economic activity. Oil prices moved up close to $40 a barrel in February, stock prices tested their lows of last fall, and consumer and business confidence ebbed. Although in January there were some signs of a post-holiday pickup in retail sales other than motor vehicles, spending was little changed, on balance, over the following three months as a gasoline price surge drained consumer purchasing power and severe winter weather kept many shoppers at home.
>
> Businesses, too, were reluctant to initiate new projects in such a highly uncertain environment. Hiring slumped, capital spending plans were put on hold, and inventories were held to very lean levels. Collectively, households and businesses hesitated to make decisions, pending news about the timing, success, and cost of military action—factors that could significantly alter the outcomes of those decisions.

Even more troubling was the fact that by the time of Greenspan's testimony, the Fed had cut short-term interest rates 12 times, from 6.5 percent to 1.25 percent, and the economy was still puzzlingly anemic.

Normally, lowering interest rates is like throwing a pork chop into a grease fire. When rates fall, companies and individuals can refinance their debts at lower rates, reducing their monthly payments, and giving them more money to spend.

The economy's sluggish behavior was even more peculiar because when the Fed lowers interest rates, it doesn't just walk out and announce that, henceforth, short-term interest rates will be lower. (Actually, it does do that, and it is a big event when the Fed makes its announcements, but that is just for informational purposes.) Instead, the Fed vastly increases the amount of money available to lend, and its actions have what are called a multiplier effect.

To push rates lower, the Fed increases the amount of money in circulation. And money, to some extent, isn't much different from fish. When six ships laden with scrod hit the docks, the price of fish falls. When there is a lot of money in the system, the price of money—interest rates—drops, too.

When the Fed lowers interest rates, it is like having an entire fleet of money-bearing ships arrive at port. To increase the money supply, the Fed buys government bonds from its primary dealers and credits the primary dealer with the purchase price. The Fed doesn't pull that cash out of a wall safe. It simply creates the cash, in the form of an electronic book entry. Viola! The money supply is now larger. The dealers now have more money on their books than they need, so they lend the excess out to other banks. But the amount they lend can be far more than the Fed gives them, thanks to the wonders of fractional banking.

Banks have to keep a certain amount of money on reserve, so they can meet withdrawals. Let's say the reserve requirement at a bank is 10 percent: For every $100 the bank lends, it must keep $10 in reserve. Now let's imagine this on a grand scale and say, for the sake of illustration, that the Fed buys $10 million in securities from one of its member banks. The bank can then lend $9 million, assuming it keeps the $1 million in reserve.

Furthermore, let's say that the bank lends $9 million to Churnem & Burnem, a retail brokerage firm. Churnem & Burnem deposits the $9 million in Fidelity Fiduciary Bank. Now Fidelity Fiduciary has $9 million in additional deposits, so it can make new loans of $8.1 million. The process repeats itself until, ultimately, much more than $10 million is loaned out.

So in May 2003, the nation was awash in money, or liquidity, as it's called on Wall Street, yet the Fed was seeing signs of economic sluggishness. It would, in June 2003, push its key fed funds rate all the way to 1 percent, a level not seen since the Fed started tracking the rate in the mid-1950s.[3] The Fed was, quite soberly, going about its job as a central bank, trying to keep the economy from falling into the abyss of a deflationary recession.

Push Me, Pull You

One of the most remarkable things about modern global finance is how frequently it invokes the law of unintended consequences. Reduce your trade barriers with China, for example, and you get cheaper toys for consumers, but you drive a toy factory in Tennessee out of business (You may also get lead poisoning). Require ethanol in gasoline and you push down oil consumption in the U.S., but you raise the price of corn around the world, and within a few months you have food riots in Mexico and the Philippines. In the case of the Federal Reserve, lowering interest rates to avoid deflation started the largest real estate boom in modern memory.

Manipulating interest rates can often have unintended consequences because it takes up to 18 months for the economy to feel the full effect of a single rate cut. To go back to our fish metaphor, suppose you ran a fish market in a mythical city. A fleet of fishing boats work far out to sea. This being the land of Mythical Examples, the only way you could communicate with this fishing fleet was to send your nephew, Fred, out to them via rowboat. If you want more fish at the market, you send Fred out to the fleet and tell them that you want more fishing boats to land at the harbor. If you want fewer fish, Fred tells some of them to take their catch to another port. Unfortunately, it takes Fred a week to get out to the fleet. Suppose one week the catch is small, and few fish arrive at the market. Prices soar. You send Fred out to summon more fishing boats. In the week that Fred's out to sea, however, the fishermen's luck improves. When the extra boats arrive, the wharf is groaning with fish, and the price has plummeted far more than you wanted.

Most times, your system works. But periodically, because of the lag, you overshoot your target, and fish prices fluctuate a bit more than you anticipated. To some extent, this is how the Fed works. Most times, monetary policy adjustments work quite well. Every once in a while, however, the Fed over-or undershoots, and things go a bit haywire. Let's just say that managing the money supply is a tricky and imperfect job at best.

As the Fed was pushing rates lower from 2000 through 2003, its interest rate changes were already working their magic on the housing market. Any increase in home prices would have been a welcome development for homeowners. And when prices did start to rise in 2000, most people saw it as a period of catch-up for a long, stagnant period of little gain.

Housing prices had barely budged in the previous decade. From January 1990 through January 2000, the Standard & Poor's/Case-Shiller home price index had gained just 2.2 percent a year.[4] During much of that period, real estate was generally ridiculed as an asset class, if only because the stock market had soared so far and so fast. The S&P 500 stock index, for example, had soared 399 percent, or 17.5 percent a year, for the same period.

To some extent, the long drought in home prices makes sense. Traditionally, real estate is the ultimate hedge against inflation, because even if your paper money becomes worthless, your house is still worth something—if only a place to sleep. And inflation in the 1990s was exceptionally low, certainly when compared with the 1970s and 1980s. But real estate had not kept up with inflation, possibly because people were too busy pouring money into the stock market in the 1990s. The consumer price index, the government's main gauge of inflation at the consumer level, rose 2.7 percent a year during the same period. So on an inflation-adjusted basis, houses were cheaper in 2000 than they were a decade earlier.

The Fed's campaign to push down short-term interest rates pulled mortgage rates down, too. This was entirely intentional: Housing is a powerful economic stimulant, and the Fed was trying to stimulate the economy. When you buy a new home, money doesn't just flow to realtors and homebuilders. You buy new furniture, new drapes, new paint, and enough lawn equipment to groom Central Park. Your home is the perfect vehicle for stimulating the economy.

And lower mortgage rates means that more people can afford more house, therefore stimulating the economy even more. Had you wanted to take out a mortgage in 2000, for example, you would have paid an average 7.5 percent in interest. The principal and interest payment on a $150,000 loan at 7.5 percent is $1,051.

By 2003, the average mortgage rate had fallen to 5.8 percent, the lowest since the Kennedy administration. At 5.8 percent, the payment on a $150,000 loan plunges to $880. Suddenly, mortgages were affordable for millions of people who had never been eligible to buy a home before.

By late 2003, the real estate market began to perk up in a big way. In Boston, for example, October home sales jumped 20 percent over October 2002. Prices had gained 7.3 percent. Real estate brokers, not known to dampen enthusiasm for a hot market, were unusually reserved. "If homeowners are realistic about price, and if their home is neat and clean, it will sell," one broker told *Boston Globe* reporter Thomas Grillo.[5]

In San Antonio, brokers noted the upsurge, too. In November—typically a quiet time for home sales, as people hunker down for Thanksgiving—brokers were seeing a flurry of activity. "This week has been like the spring rush," said Randy White, an agent at Prudential Texas Properties' Southlake office, to Andrea Jares, reporter for the *San Antonio Star-Telegram*. "It's not just me, I think it's the market."[6]

In California, the fall slump turned into an autumn wonderland for realtors. October home sales hit their highest level since October 1988 in Los Angeles. And, according to the *Los Angeles Times*, prices were soaring, too:

> "Home sale prices in October also kept growing at a sizzling pace," reporter Karen Robinson-Jacobs wrote. "The median price in Los Angeles County climbed 22% from a year ago to about $332,000 last month, although prices dipped from September's median price of $336,000." In Orange County, median home prices hit a new record of about $440,000, a 19% increase from a year ago, and up 2% from September's median sale price of $431,000.[7]

All in all, the *Miami Herald* noted, 2003 was a record-setting year for the real estate industry:

> Almost everything clicked: Annual records were set in the numbers and dollar volume of resales of existing houses, sales of new homes and the dollar volume of new home mortgages made by residential lenders.
>
> Mortgage interest rates hit 40-year lows and, more important, stayed there for the entire year. Appreciation rates in the values of existing homes moderated, but in many parts of the country they were still three to five times higher than the growth of the core Consumer Price Index—the national measure of inflation in all goods and services.[8]

By the end of 2003, home prices had gained 8 percent nationwide, their best showing since 1953. Even so, for the

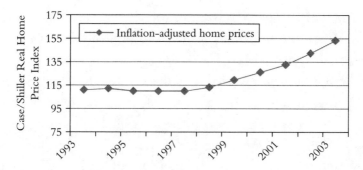

Figure 2.1   Inflation-adjusted Home Prices

10 years since 1993, prices had gained an average of just 3.2 percent a year. By most accounts, the recent good fortunes of the housing market were a long-overdue rise—and entirely predictable, given lower mortgage rates. (See Figure 2.1)

The Humble Mortgage

The second element of the housing boom was the basic 30-year fixed-rate mortgage. It is, perhaps, the last place on earth you would expect to find mild opprobrium, much less slack-jawed, eye-popping mania. Few investments are more innocent and sensible than the humble mortgage. In it conventional form—30 years, fixed rate—the mortgage is a true example of finance working to make the lives of its men and women better.

Mortgages are loans secured by property. The origin of the word comes from the French for "dead pledge." It doesn't mean that someone kills you when you default, or that you won't pay off the loan before you die, even though that may well be true. The origin of the word is legalistic: When the borrower repays the loan, the property is dead to the lender. He cannot take it back. When the borrower defaults on the loan, the property is dead to the borrower.[9]

Early mortgages were simply five- or ten-year interest-only loans that had a large—and usually unrepayable—principal payment at the end. (These loans are called balloon payments now). Also, often mortgage loans were callable, meaning that the lender could demand repayment in full under certain conditions. The odds were stacked in favor of the lender, and not in a good way.

These loan features gave birth to the moustache-twirling movie villains in early movies, parodied by Snidely Whiplash, archenemy of Dudley Do-Right in the eponymous 1960s cartoon. Snidely was continually threatening to repossess the home of the beautiful Nell, who nearly always wound up tied to the railroad tracks. Dudley invariably rescued her.

We laugh at it now. But the fact remained that most people were unable to own their homes at the turn of the 19th century. Just 46.5 percent of households owned their own home in 1900; that fell to 45.9 percent in 1920. During the 1920s, however, rising economic prosperity—particularly in the farm belt—pushed homeownership to 47.8 percent by 1930.[10]

But the Great Depression forced a revolution in how Americans bought homes. As the economy slumped, foreclosures soared. Borrowers couldn't keep up with their mortgage payments and banks had to auction off properties to stay solvent. Entire towns of dispossessed families, called "Hoovervilles," sprung up in vacant lots or on the edge of town. Washington, D.C. had a Hooverville of 15,000 in the Anacostia section of town, composed mainly of World War I veterans. The encampment was demolished by the U.S. Army, led by Gen. Douglas McArthur, Major Dwight Eisenhower, and Gen. George Patton.[11]

At some foreclosure auctions, the entire community would turn out and make sure that bids wouldn't rise above a few cents. At these "penny auctions," anyone who bid more than a few dollars usually got a tap on the shoulder from a six-foot-five farmer, who would say, casually, "Say, that bid's little high, ain't it?"[12] The idea, of course, was to keep the price so low that the bank couldn't afford to take the auction price.

Because of foreclosures, popular opinion against banks rose so high that bank robbers like Pretty Boy Floyd became folk heroes. Floyd robbed more than a dozen Midwest banks before he was gunned down by police in East Liverpool, Ohio. He was taken home to Oklahoma to be buried, and his funeral remains the largest in Oklahoma history. On a less violent note, consider the perennial Christmas movie, *It's a Wonderful Life.* Mr. Potter, the evil banker, worked to thwart the Building and Loan, a far more democratic way of lending. (As an inside joke, Potter's rental development is called Potter's Field—a term for a pauper's graveyard.)

The rash of foreclosures—particularly farm foreclosures, which hit nearly 20,000 a month[13]—quickly became a political issue, and worked its way in to Franklin Roosevelt's 1932 campaign platform.[14]

As president, Roosevelt created the Home Owner's Loan Corporation, which refinanced troubled mortgages. The HOLC took short-term mortgage loans and refinanced them to longer-term loans. The HOLC loans had another important difference: They were fully amortized, which means that borrowers repaid

principal and interest over the course of the loan, in effect elim-
inating the need for a balloon payment.

The HOLC could refinance home loans up to $20,000,
which is the equivalent of $328,500 today. It also refinanced
problem loans for lenders, helping inject much-needed funds
into the lending market and keeping many banks solvent. The
HOLC stopped making loans in 1935, and eventually paid
back the money the government had given it, plus a modest
profit.[15]

But its legacy—the long-term, fully amortized mortgage
loan—was arguably the biggest leap forward in finance for the
average person. By extending a mortgage's payment period and
spreading out interest and principal payments, houses became
much more affordable. Homeownership, helped by loan pro-
grams by the Veterans Administration, rose to 55 percent in
1950 and 66 percent by 2000. The 30-year mortgage, in short,
is a Good Thing.

Of course, no financial arrangement is immune to greed.
Before the great mortgage collapse of 2007 was the great mortgage meltdown of 1989—which is ironic, because mortgage
lending is a license to make money. Lots of money. You won't
make the same kind of money that you would if you invented
an anti-gravity machine or discovered a way to generate elec-
tricity from old tires. But you can make lots of money in the
mortgage business, nonetheless.

Before 1982, the government set the maximum rate that
banks could pay in interest. Banks would proudly advertise
that they paid "the maximum rate allowed by law"—about
5 percent by early 1982. The law made it hard for banks to pay
depositors more than the bank received in interest.

But by 1981, you could buy a three-month Treasury bill that would pay you 10 percent. Consumers pulled their deposits from banks and fled to Treasury securities or money market mutual funds, which invested in Treasury securities and other short-term debts. In response to the strangled screams of bankers, Congress lifted the limits on what banks could pay for deposits in 1982. Banks could now compete for deposits, by offering higher interest rates.

All well and good. Here again, however, the law of unintended consequences kicked in. Small, ambitious banks and savings and loans found they could offer very high deposit rates and attract lots of deposits, particularly if they used national deposit brokers, who, for a commission, would round up willing depositors. To make money from these high-interest deposits, however, the S&Ls had to make risky loans. After all, the riskier the loan, the higher the return. If you were to lend money to General Electric, for example, you would probably ask for a relatively low interest rate because GE has tons of cash. If you were to lend money to your no-good cousin Billy, however, you would probably charge a high interest rate, because Billy is not only constantly broke, but has a weakness for the horses.

S&Ls then made progressively riskier loans, often overlooking such niceties as the borrower's capacity to repay those loans. And, because real estate was frothy in those days, they figured that the value of the collateral would rise enough to cushion them against any defaults.

The result was the largest banking collapse in history, followed by the largest taxpayer-funded bailout in history. The savings and loan crisis cost the government more than $1 trillion.

The collapse of Home State Savings Bank in Ohio caused the governor to declare a bank holiday—something not seen since the Great Depression. The failure of Lincoln Savings led to five U.S. senators being rebuked—among them Senators John Glenn and John McCain. And the collapse of Silverado Savings and Loan led to Neil Bush, President Bush's brother, being fined $50,000 by the Federal Deposit Insurance Corp.

By the end of the savings and loan debacle, not one major bank in Texas was left standing. Most banks in Massachusetts were wiped out, too. The Federal Deposit Insurance Corp., which oversees state-chartered banks, developed a major high-speed, over-the-weekend SWAT-style method of closing troubled banks and, if not liquidating them outright, merging them with another bank. When you made a deposit on Friday, you could never be quite sure what your bank's name would be on Monday.

By the mid-1990s, the savings and loan industry was a shadow of its former self. The Federal Savings and Loan Insurance Corp., the FDIC's counterpart for thrifts, vanished entirely.

One would think that the banking industry would have learned its lesson. One would be wrong, as we will see in the next chapter.

Package Them Up and Move Them Out

The final ingredient for the housing bubble of 2000 was the mortgage-backed security. It, too, had a fairly innocuous beginning.

Let's start with the notion that a mortgage, like most other debts, is negotiable—that is, it can be bought and sold. Those who create mortgages, such as banks and credit unions, are the *primary* mortgage market. Those who buy existing mortgages are the *secondary* mortgage market.

Although people have been buying and selling mortgages for ages the modern secondary mortgage market also begins with the Roosevelt administration—in particular, with the Federal National Mortgage Association, best known by its Wall Street nickname, Fannie Mae.

One problem during the Depression was that banks became afraid to lend money for mortgages—or much else for that matter. They had simply lost too much money because of defaults. Creating mortgages and holding them for the long term was a bit like jumping rope in a mine field. Sooner or later—probably sooner—something bad was going to happen.

On the other hand, there's always a market for high-quality investments that pay regular income—such as mortgages, for example. A safe investment that makes regular interest payments is particularly attractive when prices are falling. If you own a bond that pays $100 interest a year, for example, your $100 will buy more goods and services each year as prices fall.

The Federal National Mortgage Corporation, of Fannie Mae, created in 1938, was designed to connect mortgage makers and mortgage buyers. Fannie Mae takes mortgages, packages them into income-bearing securities, and sells them to institutional investors, such as mutual funds and pension funds.

By buying and packaging loans, Fannie Mae helps make sure there is plenty of mortgage money to lend. Consider a bank that makes 100 mortgages. It could, if it wanted, hold the mortgages and collect the interest. But it also has the option of selling all or some of them. If it sold all 100 to Fannie Mae, it would then have money on hand to make another 100 mortgages. (Rival

Freddie Mac, or the Federal Home Loan Mortgage Corporation, was created by Congress in 1970 to give Fannie Mae some competition.)

In order to package and sell the mortgages, however, Fannie Mae had to insist on certain lending standards. For one reason, in the financial world, as in the supermarket, customers insist on knowing what they are buying. It's really not much different than buying fish.

Suppose you owned a restaurant, and you wanted to buy some fish for tonight's specials. You probably wouldn't say to the fish dealer, "Send me a big bag of fish. Whatever you have on hand. I just want some fish."

You would ask, instead, for, say, 50 pounds of salmon, 20 of cod, another 35 of flounder. And you would also specify the quality: You might get a good discount on day-old fish, but you probably wouldn't want it. Nor would you want to pick out starfish, minnows and old bottles of suntan lotion from your bag of fish. It's always good to be specific. Similarly, an investor on Wall Street probably won't say, "Give me a big old sack of mortgages. I don't care if it's a loan on a refrigerator box to the local homeless guy or to Donald Trump's newest hotel. I just want me some mortgages."

So Fannie Mae sets certain guidelines for the mortgages it packages. Currently, for example, Fannie Mae limits loan purchases on single-family homes to $417,000 per mortgage.[16] (There are higher limits for Alaska, Hawaii, Guam, and the U.S. Virgin Islands, where home prices tend to be considerably higher than those on the mainland.)

Fannie Mae also requires that the borrower be able to display a minimum level of income and have a decent history of repaying debts. The company guarantees timely principal and interest payments to investors who buy its packages or mortgages, so these requirements don't matter much to investors. The guidelines matter a great deal to Fannie Mae, however. Companies that make guarantees hate to actually have to honor them. By setting lending standards, Fannie Mae reduces the risk of having to shell out extra money for defaulted mortgages. (The company also levies a guaranty fee, which helps ease its pain a bit.)

Over time, mortgage packages have become immensely popular with investors, particularly institutional investors. Typically, mortgages yield about two percentage points more than the yield on 10-year Treasury securities. A fund manager or pension manager who wanted to get a bit of extra yield could buy a mortgage-backed security, instead.

Packages of mortgages guaranteed by Ginnie Mae, the nickname for the Goverment National Mortgage Association, packages Mortgages made by the Federal Housing Adminstration, the Veterans Administration, and others are particularly popular: The U.S. government guarantees timely interest and principal payments on the mortgages in the package. About 50 mutual funds specialize in Ginnie Mae securities, and mortgages form the backbone of many pension-fund and insurance company portfolios, too.

The Big Bear

Before we continue with the collapse of Bear Stearns we need to set the scene with one other piece: How Bear Stearns and the Wall Street investment banking industry work.

Investment banks are far different from the types of banks that make mortgages. An investment bank's main business is bringing new securities to market.

Suppose, for example, you owned Acme Fish. In order to raise $10 million, you would need to sell 30 percent of your company to the public.

You can't just hawk stock on the street corner, however. You need to make certain disclosures to potential investors, such as how much money you make, how you make it, and where you invest your earnings. You have to file for permission to sell the stock to the public through the Securities and Exchange Commission.

More importantly, you have to sell the stock. You have to make sure that brokers know the stock is available. You would like them to be excited about selling the stock. And you would have to know how much to charge per share at its initial offering price.

So you pick up the phone and call your investment banker. For a fee, of course, he will make sure you get your paperwork done properly, and advise you on the initial price of Acme Fish stock.

Typically, the investment bank will then take on the task of underwriting the stock, or selling it to the public. Sometimes, the bank will buy the stock outright—typically for less than what it thinks the market price will be—and will take on full responsibility for selling the stock to the public.

Other times, it will hold a Dutch auction, which means the bidding for the stock starts with a high price and lowers it until someone starts buying. The Dutch, incidentally, call this a Chinese auction, while the Chinese call it an Irish auction. (Or sometimes the underwriter simply pledges to do its best to sell all or most of the stock.)

Bear Stearns was not the world's largest investment bank, nor was it the oldest, but by the 1980s it had become a formidable player in the field. The company was founded in 1923 by Joseph Bear, Robert Stearns, and Harold Mayer. Noted for aggressive trading, Bear Stearns always had a patina of street smarts, rather than an air of old money. If you were a tough trader from Brooklyn—or Des Moines, for that matter—Bear would take you on.

Bear's chairman from 1978 to 1993, Alan (Ace) Greenberg, is widely credited with building Bear from a scrappy trading house to a major investment bank. Greenberg, a highly regarded bridge player, pushed Bear Stearns into the mortgage-backed securities business. The company went public in 1985.

Greenberg's associate (and sometime bridge partner) Jimmy Cayne succeeded him in 1985, although Greenberg continued to work as chairman of Bear's executive committee.

By 2006, Bear was the fifth-largest investment bank in the country. More than 15,000 employees worked for the company at its offices, scattered from New York to Mumbai. The company had $67 billion in capital and assets of $350 billion. Bear Stearns stock traded for $150 per share; Wall Street valued the company's outstanding stock at $23.2 billion. Most importantly, it was a primary dealer in government securities, one of just 20 companies that trade directly with the Federal Reserve System.

So, at least initially, the U.S. had a well-functioning system for the real estate market. A working person could get a loan for a reasonably priced home from a bank. The bank, in turn, could sell the mortgage to Wall Street, and Wall Street investment bankers could sell a package of mortgages to investors. It was a highly functioning, well-evolved system—until things started to get bubbly in 2003.

Chapter 3

Silly Season

Alfred Nobel, scion of a Swedish factory owner (his father had invented plywood), gained his enormous fortune by solving an especially difficult problem. The problem was this: Nitroglycerine, which had been discovered by a school chum of his, was a marvelously compact explosive. It was much easier to lug around than kegs of gunpowder, it wasn't terribly sensitive to water, and it had far more explosive capability than gunpowder did.

Unfortunately, nitroglycerine was also very unstable. A sudden shock—dropping it, for example—could dispatch a clumsy assistant straight to Copenhagen, without benefit of a boat. Nobel had to figure out how to stabilize it, so that it could be conveniently transported. And he did, by mixing nitro with diatomaceous earth and sodium carbonate. The result was dynamite, which could be rolled into handy tubes and transported fairly safely.

Our friend Mr. Dynamite can be used for good or evil. It can break rock instantly, saving workers (or convicts) thousands of hours of tedious labor, or demolish an old building in a minute, saving weeks of demolition time. In the wrong hands—say, of the Mad Bomber, who terrorized New York for nearly a decade—it can cause chaos and suffering and untold human misery.

In Nobel's life, dynamite provided the money for the Nobel Prize; it also took the life of his brother, Emil, in 1864.

Well, you can always figure out a way to make something innocent into something bad; you can turn a leg of frozen lamb into an Easter dinner or a murder weapon, if you're so inclined. And so it is with a financial tool called leverage.

In its most basic sense, leverage simply means using borrowed money to invest. Leverage has two distinct advantages. For one thing, it can greatly amplify your gains, if you bet correctly. For another, if you completely botch things up, you've lost other people's money, not your own. (OPM, or Other People's Money, is an important concept on Wall Street, one which Bear Stearns used rather freely, as we shall see.)

Let's look at a simple example, one that is used every day by homeowners. Suppose you decide to buy a house for $150,000. Unfortunately, you don't have $150,000 cooling its heels in your checking account. You do, however, know someone who does have money, and is willing to lend it to you—your banker.

You're seeking a conventional loan, which means that you have to put down 20 percent, or $30,000, of your own money. Fortunately, you do have that. So you pay the seller $30,000, and friendly Mr. Banker lends you an additional $120,000. Time goes by, and after a decade, you decide to sell. Much to your delight, your first offer comes in at $225,000. You pay

Mr. Banker $120,000, and you have $105,000 in your account. You've turned $30,000 into $105,000—a 250 percent gain. Had you paid all cash for the house, you would have made a 50 percent gain.

Now, this is a simple illustration, one that's disregarding the interest paid to Mr. Banker over the years, as well as the taxes and the cost of buying new drapes, new fencing, and that Toro mower. On the other hand, whenever people make a lot of money on a house, they disregard all those things, anyway. They just see that big pot of cash in their bank account.

And as the spring selling season began in 2004, many people were seeing big pots of cash when they sold their houses. Suddenly, the newspapers were full of headlines like these:

- Home prices up, up, up: Single-family median at record high in November—*San Francisco Chronicle,* Dec. 17, 2004
- In L.A. real estate, $10 million is the new $1 million—*Los Angeles Times,* August 29, 2004
- Housing on a wild ride; prices hitting new records, causing worries—*New York Times,* November 14, 2004

According to the *Boston Globe,* a parking space at the Brimmer Garage downtown sold for $160,000. A single space sold for $27,000 in 1998.[1]

Irrational Exuberance?

Some observers were beginning to sense that this was more than your average housing rally. One person who was particularly interested in the real estate market was Yale economist Robert Shiller. Shiller was the author of a book published in

2000, called *Irrational Exuberance.* In it—and with exquisite timing—he set out to prove that the technology bubble of the 1990s was, in fact, a bubble. (It seems hard to believe it now, but Wall Street generally thought Shiller's opinion was far too much of a Chicken Little approach. Technology, after all, was the future.)

In the second edition of his book, Shiller examined real estate prices and came to another heretical conclusion: By and large, you don't get rich off real estate. Home prices tend to muddle along for long periods of time, suddenly rise, and then go nowhere for another long period of time. By and large, he argued, home prices remain a fairly stable percentage of peoples' incomes.

What he had discovered about the real estate market of the middle of this decade was considered heresy by virtually everyone in the real estate market: That prices, adjusted for income, were higher than they had ever been, and higher than they should be. The argument, in essence, was this: When prices get too high, people start to move elsewhere. Eventually, "elsewhere" becomes desirable in its own right. In the Washington, D.C. area, for example, many people now commute to Tyson's Corner, once a desolate crossroads with a gas station and an apple stand.

In other words, the availability of wide open spaces is probably the worst enemy of real estate. And, although realtors are fond of saying that they don't make any more real estate, there's plenty of wide open spaces in the U.S. While Shiller had achieved some respect and notoriety for his call on the technology bubble, the notion of a housing bubble was met with skepticism, particularly by the housing industry, which accused him of being a publicity hound.

The Federal Reserve Board of New York published a paper in April 2001 by Jonathan McCarthy and Richard Peach, which found "little basis for such concerns. The marked upturn in home prices is largely attributable to strong market fundamentals: Home prices have essentially moved in line with increases in family income and declines in nominal mortgage interest rates." In other words, the Fed wasn't buying the bubble argument.

But soon Professor Shiller wasn't the only one using the word "bubble" to describe the real estate market. Increasingly, the term was being used in real estate roundups in daily newspapers, followed by the observation that all real estate is local, and therefore a national bubble was impossible.

Perhaps, but the national market certainly was inflating. The national Case-Shiller index gained 16.6 percent from March 2004 through March 2005, and some areas had soared much higher. In Las Vegas, home prices shot up 33 percent. In San Francisco, prices jumped 23 percent. Washington, D.C. recorded an average 26 percent gain.

And in California, Florida, Boston, Washington, New York, and Chicago, neighbors were talking about home prices. Mr. Smith sold his house for $400,000! Mrs. Jones got $50,000 more than the asking price! Prospective buyers were advised that the asking price was just a starting point for the action, not a number you were supposed to talk people down from.

Let's take a look at a property in Herndon, Virginia, a small community in the northwest Washington, D.C. suburbs. Herndon was a small dairy farming community founded, in large part by Union Civil War veterans who found the climate hospitable. (It is one of the few towns in Virginia that can boast a Grant street.)

The town began to grow in the 1960s, when a small development called Chandon Woods was built. The houses were modest split-level ranches or ramblers with quarter-acre lots. The street names had a Southern bent: Florida, Arkansas, Alabama (and, inexplicably, Pickett).

In 1971, 408 Pickett Lane—named after the general who led Pickett's charge at Gettysburg—sold for $30,000. As Washington boomed in the 1980s and 1990s, Herndon did, too, growing from a sleepy village to a bedroom suburb. The house values went up sharply as the town grew, averaging a bit less than 8 percent appreciation a year.

In 2001, however, 408 Pickett became a gold mine. Fairfax County appraised the home at $139,150, up 15 percent from $121,000 in 2000. But the best was yet to come. The next year, 2002, the county assessed the home at $173,660, a 24.8 percent jump. The following year, 2003, the house's tax value jumped another 15 percent, to $199,710. By 2004, the Herndon market—or Fairfax County's assessment of it—cooled a bit. The county marked up the value of 408 Pickett lane just 10 percent, to $219,680.

But 2005 seems to have been a watershed year, at least for Herndon real estate. That year, Fairfax judged the house to be worth $282,880, a 28.77 percent increase. But apparently, the county assessor lowballed the property: It changed hands that year for $400,000, more than $100,000 more than its appraised value. And at that, it was a bit of a bargain. Down the road a bit, 417 Pickett sold in 2005 for $445,000. It had sold in 2001 for $247,000. And across the street, 409 Pickett Lane, a three-bedroom rambler with a pool and garage, sold for $510,000. It had been purchased in 1998 for $164,900.

Across the country in Los Angeles, homeowners were see-ing similar rises. Lynwood, a community formed in 1913 along the rail line to Santa Anna, was named after a nearby dairy and creamery. Today it's a largely Latino neighborhood, and the median income is about $41,000.

Let's let the *L.A. Times* tell the story about the Lynnwood housing market here:

Another area that saw prices soar *was Lynwood 90262, where the median price per square foot shot up 19.8% in the latter half of 2004.*

That's good news for Lynwood homeowner Hodges Pittman, 67, a retired plumber, but not for his nephew, Rodney Cooper, 42, a ramp agent for Southwest Airlines who, despite steady employment, has seen homeownership slip further from his grasp.

Taking a break from fertilizing the lawn in front of the Shirley Avenue house that Pittman's family purchased in 1969 for $24,000, uncle and nephew ruminated on changes in the neighborhood.

"I'm saving and I had a two-year plan, but that's changed a little bit," Cooper said. "I thought prices would come down, but they keep going up."

What he's increasingly seeing, Pittman said, are fami-lies pooling their resources to buy and share homes in the neighborhood.

"A house across the street sold for $400,000, and it wasn't even one of the nicer houses in the neighborhood," he said. "The average income around here is about $30,000 or $40,000—and that's two people working. How is someone like that going to afford a $400,000 home?"[2]

Soon, "flipping" became a national pastime: You buy a house, make a few quick fixes, and sell it for a much higher price shortly thereafter. In parts of Las Vegas in 2005, for example, 52.3 percent of home sales were flipped in 12 months.[3] You could find out how to flip houses through books like *Find it, Fix it, Flip it! Make Millions in Real Estate—One House At A Time* or the inevitable *Flipping Houses for Dummies*.

Eventually, flipping even extended to homes that hadn't been built yet. Investors would pledge to buy a new home and sell the home before the foundations had been poured. In Boston, more than 10 percent of new condos were purchased by speculators. At Porter 156, an old light-bulb factory in East Boston, an investor flipped a condo for $439,000, more than $100,000 over her purchase price. "There are a huge number of flippers," she said. "If I didn't close quickly, I would be up against 30 or 40 units in a matter of a week."[4]

It wasn't just Boston. As early as 2004, as many as 50 percent of condo buyers in Miami-Dade county were investors, few of whom actually expected to spend a night in the property.[5]

Naturally, Wall Street got in on the act, too. The stock prices of homebuilders soared in 2004 and 2005. Toll Brothers stock peaked at $58.70 in July 2005, after soaring 180 percent the previous 12 months. Rival Ryland Homes jumped more than 100 percent the same period. In some areas, home construction was so hot that people gave up technology jobs to swing a hammer.

The major homebuilders confidently assured the public that, unlike every other housing boom, this time was different: They wouldn't overbuild and be left with vast amounts of unsold inventory. When asked about the possibility of a slowing housing market in 2005, Robert Toll, CEO of Toll Brothers, said, "It means you don't raise the prices as fast as you raised them in the last year and a half, which means you don't make more money than you are currently making. You're still making a bushel full, but the bushel doesn't become a ton."[6]

Banks Break out the Levers

One question naturally comes to mind as we ponder the great housing bubble: Where did all those buyers get all that money? It's simple. They borrowed it.

Initially, the housing bubble was borne on a wave of conventional loans, the kind that Fannie Mae and Freddie Mac make routinely. People found that they could sell their old homes at a profit and buy newer, bigger houses. They would simply take out a conventional mortgage with a higher down payment. It's the American way.

Many borrowers, too, refinanced their mortgages at lower interest rates—normally, a smart personal financial move, provided you plan to stay in the house. Your lower payments quickly make up for any closing costs, and you have extra money to spend, save, or invest.

Because home prices had soared so high, however, many people refinanced their mortgages for more than their initial loan—an option called the cash-out refi. For example, if you owed $150,000 on your mortgage, you could take out a new mortgage at, say, $180,000. You'd get a check for $30,000 and your payments would stay roughly the same, because interest rates were lower. In the first quarter of 2005, 64 percent of loans owned by Freddie Mac were refinanced for loan amounts that were at least 5 percent higher than the original amount.

The pace doubled in the second quarter of 2005. Homeowners took $59 billion in cash from their homes, double the amount a year earlier, according to Freddie Mac. Fully 74 percent of new refinancings were cash-out refis. Many saw this as a good thing. All this new cash, for example, allowed people to put on additions, make home repairs—even buy new cars.

But there's a limit to the number of people who can do that. And as prices rose, new buyers simply started getting priced out of the market. By the first quarter of 2004, 80 metropolitan areas tracked by the National Association of Realtors reported above-average gains in home prices, and 35 reported double-digit gains, according to *USA Today*.[7]

Reports of bidding wars over properties started trickling into the news. In Los Angeles, realtors became used to getting 10 bids or more on a single property. The winning bid typically topped the asking price by $50,000 or more.[8] As prices soared, it became harder and harder for first-time buyers to get into the housing market. Normally, this is what cools off the housing market: The pool of potential buyers shrinks, homes stay on the market longer, and prices begin to fall.

But the true frenzy had one more stage left. Buyers who were squeezed out of desirable downtown locations started to move to the suburbs; those who couldn't afford the suburbs settled for the exurbs, where prices were lower. Other people decided not to buy a house at all, but rather a more affordable condominium.

But there's another way to make housing more affordable, and that's to fiddle with financing. Here again, this has a long

history, and a generally well-intentioned one. Many return-
ing soldiers from World War II and Korea, for example, were
given the chance to buy a home with no money down, thanks
to government-guaranteed VA mortgages. (Banks back then
were sober enough to want borrowers to have some skin in
the game. Failing that, they were pleased to take a government
guarantee.) Although buyers built up equity slowly, it enabled
an entire generation of soldiers to buy their first homes.

And in California, where home prices have always been
higher than the national average, lenders rolled out a new, popular
type of mortgage in the 1970s and 1980s called the adjustable-rate
mortgage, or ARM. Rather than having a fixed rate for 30 years,
the interest rate on an ARM would change every year, according
to market conditions.

Bankers loved ARMs because it shifted interest-rate risk from
them to consumers. Banks borrow money at short-term rates
from depositors and lend it out for 30 years. Normally, long-
term rates are higher than short-term rates. But sometimes, when
short-term rates spike up, a bank is stuck paying depositors as much
as 7 percent while collecting 6 percent on their loans, and the difference is the bank's profit. In banking terms, this is a Bad Thing.

A bank that owned an ARM didn't have to worry if rates
suddenly soared, because the rates on its mortgage portfolio
would rise, too. All the bank had to worry about was whether
or not the borrower was financially sound enough to repay his
debt. The public usually liked ARMs, too, because their initial
rates were lower than a traditional 30-year loan rate. An ARM
could be a good way for a first-time buyer to get into a home.
Back in the early 1980s, when double-digit mortgage rates
were common, you could sometimes get an initial ARM rate

at 9 percent or so—a rate considered a darn good bargain back in the day.

Here again, having lending conventions helped. Early ARMs could rise as high as interest rates did—which was extraordinarily high in the 1970s and 1980s. Unwary borrowers could sign a note with an initial rate of 6 percent and, two years later, be saddled with a 14 percent note. Eventually—and with some regulatory prodding—the industry settled on a fairly standard mortgage that would allow the rate to rise at the most 2 percent a year, to a maximum 6 percentage points over the original rate.

As prices rose in 2003 and 2004, however, even ARMs weren't enough to keep new buyers in the market. Lenders had to find new ways to make payments affordable. And they did. One easy way to make a house more affordable is to simply stretch out the payments over a longer period of time. For example, car companies often tout low interest rates on auto loans, but to be honest, the rate doesn't make a huge amount of difference on a short-term loan. For example, suppose you take out a three-year auto loan at 5 percent. Your monthly payment will be $450. At 2 percent, your payment would be $430—$20 a month lower. Woo.

But let's say you took a 5 percent loan for five years. Your payment would drop to $283, a considerable difference. This is why the loan financing department of your local car dealer has become a major sales center—and profit center, too.

Expanding the payment period for cars also makes the payments more affordable. The same is true for a mortgage. A 30-year loan at 6 percent for a $300,000 mortgage would set you back $1,800 a month in interest and principal. Stretch the loan out to 40 years, however, and your loan payment drops to $1,650.

Even so, 40-year loans really didn't give enough of a payment drop to catch on. What lenders needed was a way to make the payment drop fantastically low—so low that a borrower of modest means could afford a vastly inflated home price.

One simple way was the interest-only loan: You paid only the interest on the loan each year for a set period, after which, you'd pay both interest and principal. The beauty of an IO loan, as it was called, was that payments were really, really, really low. For example, suppose you were eyeing a $300,000 home. Your mortgage lender could offer you a three-year IO loan, and your initial monthly payment would be just $937.50.

Now, your lender would carefully explain to you that after three years, your payments would shoot to $1,800 a month. But by then, he'd say with a chuckle, your house would have gained 50 percent in value, and you could simply refinance at more favorable rates. Or your nonworking spouse could start working. Or you could sell a kidney. Whatever. Just sign.

Of course, there is one other way you can get a borrower into a loan that he might not qualify for. You can just— nudge, nudge—not inquire too closely about the applicant's finances. After all, it's a busy world. Who's got time to check employment, or assets? You can get a "low-doc" loan, which, as its name implies, requires very little paperwork at all from the borrower. Even better, you could ask for a "no-doc" loan, which basically requires an earnest demeanor.

Eventually, banks started offering NINA loans—no income, no assets—meaning that a quick glance at your credit score was all that was really required. *National Public Radio* and *This*

American Life found a borrower who exemplified the NINA loan: Clarence Nathan, who earned $45,000 a year and got a $540,000 loan. "I wouldn't have loaned me the money, and nobody that I know would have loaned me the money," Nathan said. "I mean, I know guys who are criminals who wouldn't lend me that money, and they'd break your kneecap."[9]

Finally, there was the little matter of a down payment. Many banks did require the borrower to have some of his own money in the deal. What if the borrower had none? One simple, but ingenious solution: Borrow it. Some borrowers would get a blended loan—the down payment would be a home equity loan, at a higher rate, and the rest would be a mortgage at a lower rate. These borrowers were levered 100 percent—a remarkable new development in the history of mortgage lending.

With such a plethora of low-payment options from which to choose, the pool of potential buyers suddenly blossomed. Why, you could buy a half-million dollar house with payments of just $2,500 a month with an interest-only ARM. Even better, the mortgage broker—the helpful fellow who presented all these options to the buyer—got a commission for making the sale. It really made no difference whether or not the borrower was actually qualified.

All of these options have many appealing features for the borrower, as well as the mortgage broker. And, of course, the availability of these loans makes real estate fever burn even hotter, which makes homeowners and realtors happy. But the next question is: Who on earth would want to lend money at these terms? Plenty of people, as it turned out.

Originating loans, even awful ones, have a significant advantage: Fees. Wonderful, lovely fees. You can collect fees for the title search, which you don't really do. Instead, you buy title insurance. You charge fees for credit checks. Fees for applications. You can charge a fee for lower rates. Charge another fee for mortgage insurance. Charge a fee for sitting down at the lender's office. Charge a fee for sitting in the chair. Charge a fee for breathing the bank's air.

Even though many companies wanted to make terrible loans—which were given the wonderful euphemism "subprime"—few lenders actually wanted to hold them in their own portfolios. Even adding in the fees, the chance of outright bankruptcy was simply too high.

Fannie Mae and Freddie Mac had standards, and generally didn't buy subprime loans. (Both companies, however, had their own woes, which we will deal with later.) But really, honestly and truly, many of these loans were pure garbage. What could you do with these dreadful loans?

Wall Street Adds a Few Levers of Its Own

And it's here that Wall Street's genius came in. Many investors love mortgage packages, such as those put together by Ginnie Mae, Fannie Mae, and Freddie Mac. Mortgages yield more than Treasury bonds, and often more than top-rated corporate bonds, too. And subprime mortgages, in theory, could earn much more.

Freddie and Fannie and Ginnie weren't the only ones packaging mortgages: Any company with the proper government permits could package debt together and sell them on Wall Street. They were called collateralized debt obligations, or CDOs, and they had been around for a long time.

Nevertheless, if you create big pools of crummy mortgages, you just have a big bunch of crummy mortgages. What Wall Street needed was a way to turn these big bundles of garbage into something that seemed sweeter.

The answer, eventually, came in the notion of the tranche, or "slice." Let's say you have a big pool of subprime mortgages. We'll call them the Blue Ridge Mortgage Pool. You know that a certain percentage of those mortgages will default. You know that because you can hire smart guys who can look at past history and estimate, to within a fraction, what percent will go bad.

Let's take one slice of the pool, and slice it this way. The buyer of this particular tranche, called Tranche A, will be guaranteed that it will only get dinged by defaults after 20 percent or more of the pool defaults. Hard to imagine that happening. And because the odds of a 20 percent default rate are so low, those who hold Tranche A get the lowest interest rate—say, a half a percentage point higher than comparable Treasuries.

Now, Tranche B will get defaults from 10 to 20 percent of the pool—admittedly, a bigger risk. But they will also get a much higher interest rate. Let's say 3 percentage points higher than Treasuries.

Tranche C—a very, very hard sell—will get defaults from 0 to 10 percent. But they will get the highest interest rate of all, a full 8 percent above Treasuries. Many times, even the best salesmen on Wall Street couldn't sell the lowest tranches, so the brokerage houses often kept them for themselves.

Risky? Sure! But there's an active market of people buying and selling these things. Whenever you feel like the market's getting a bit too scary, you can sell them to someone else. A bigger fool, as it were.

Nevertheless, many institutional investors—the target market for packages of subprime mortgages—aren't fools. In addition, many have strict guidelines over what kinds of debt they can and can't buy. You wouldn't want your pension fund investing in a package of Uncle Harry's gambling debts, for example.

Typically, an institutional investor will have a restriction on the credit quality of the bonds or notes it can buy. Although bond funds and pension funds employ legions of analysts to decide the risk of default on a bond issue, they also look for some help from outside sources—most notably, the bond ratings agencies. Many investors, for example, will only buy bonds with top ratings from agencies, and many more won't buy poorly rated ones.

Moody's Investors Service was—and still is—one of the premier bond rating agencies. The company was founded in 1900 by John Moody, an entrepreneur who published a manual of debt securities. The book was an instant hit—on Wall Street anyway—and after a two-year hiatus because of the Panic of 1907, came back with a new idea: A debt rating service. For a fee, subscribers could get Moody's concise opinion on the creditworthiness of various corporate bonds.

The company's main rival is Standard & Poor's, formed in 1941 by a merger between Standard Statistics and Poor's Publishing. It also rates securities. For a long time, the two companies rated whichever securities they liked, and those who wanted to know the companies' opinions had to pay them. Several decades ago, the companies began charging companies to rate their debt.

The practice brings an interesting interplay between the debt issuer and the debt rates. Issuers typically want the highest possible rating for their debt, because that gives them the larg-est potential pool of buyers. So in many cases, the issuer will work closely with the rater to see what safeguards it can use to get the highest possible rating.

In the case of the subprime-backed bonds, many of the top tranches earned the highest possible ratings from Moody's and Standard and Poor's, which enabled the bonds' creators to sell them to a vast pool of institutional buyers around the globe.

So, in a nutshell, our story stands here. Banks, eager to make new loans, began to make increasingly creative loans to increas-ingly shaky borrowers. These subprime loans were packaged by Wall Street investment banks, sliced into different tranches, some of which earned AAA ratings from the world's most respected ratings agencies. These slices of subprime goodness were then sold to investors all around the world. Surely, there couldn't be any way to make these investments any more risky, could there? Of course there could. Leverage isn't limited to buying real estate. You can also use leverage to invest in stocks or bonds.

Back in the Roaring Twenties, you could buy stocks at shady brokerages, called bucket shops, with 10 percent down or less. Your friendly broker would lend you the remainder, with interest, of course.

Borrowed money is a thing of beauty in a rip-snorting bull market like the one in the 1920s. Let's say that you were a smart young chap and noticed that all your friends were listen-ing to a newfangled device called the radio. So you did a bit of research and discovered that RCA Radio—in the broker par-lance of the day—sold for $10 a share.

Unfortunately, you only had $100. If the company rose 10 percent—a tidy gain—you'd have just $10 in profit, a heady sum in the Roaring Twenties, but still just ten bucks. So you trot on down to your local bucket shop and buy 100 shares of Radio. Now your account is worth $1,000—$900 from the bucket shop, and $100 out of your own pocket.

You had bought stock on margin, the brokerage term for leverage. Your broker's loan was, and still is, called a margin loan—essentially a loan collateralized by securities.

Fortune smiles and Radio goes to $11 a share—a 10 percent gain. Your stake is now worth $1,100, and you sell.

You repay the bucket shop its $900 margin loan, leaving you with $100 in profit and your original $100. Even though Radio has gained just 10 percent, you've doubled your money, thanks to the joy of leverage.

Now, let's suppose the trade had gone against you. Radio shares fell to $9. Had you sold at $9, your $100 would have disappeared into your broker's coffers. You would have been ruined, do you hear? Ruined!

Before you had been completely wiped out, however, you would have gotten a margin call. This a cold, unfriendly notice from your broker that you'd better come down to the bucket shop, pronto, bringing enough cash to bring your account balances up to the maintenance requirement, or the broker will unceremoniously dump the shares at whatever price he can get.

Lending at such low collateral to loan value is risky business, as brokers found out when Wall Street laid an egg during the 1929 market crash. Although we were taught that many banks went under during the Big One, many brokerages did too, taking their clients' money with them.

But it wasn't just bucket shops that got drained. Some of the biggest brokerage firms on Wall Street got badly beaten, too, and not because they were handing out margin loans with 10 percent collateral. They went much, much further. We learned this the hard way in 2008; we also learned it in 1932, but apparently forgot. It's a story that bears interesting similarities to our present dilemma.

Once Wall Street gets an idea, it tends to take it to whatever extremes it can. In the 1920s, the extreme example was the Goldman Sachs Trading Company, a mutual fund that often bought and sold stocks on margin. The fund, designed to give the public the benefit of Goldman's vast investment expertise, was extraordinarily popular—so much so that if the fund's holdings were worth $50 a share, investors would pay $100 per share for it. Goldman then created another fund, the Shenandoah fund, which also invested in margin. The Goldman Sachs Trading Company owned shares of Shenandoah, so an investor in the Trading Company was, in effect, buying double-margined stocks. And, as a kind of icing on the cake, Shenandoah then created the Blue Ridge fund, in effect using triple margin.

The end came in the Great Crash, and is best summed up in the testimony during the inevitable Senate hearings afterwards:

Senator Couzens: "Did Goldman Sachs organize the Goldman Sachs Trading Corp.?"

Mr. Sachs: "Yes, sir."

Senator Couzens: "And sold its stock to the public?"

Mr. Sachs: "Yes, sir."

Senator Couzens: "At what price?"

Mr. Sachs: "At 104. The stock was split 2-for-1."

Senator Couzens: "And what is the price of the stock now?"

Mr. Sachs: "Approximately 1 3/4."

In the wake of the Great Crash, margin borrowing wasn't outlawed, but it was sharply curtailed. The Federal Reserve sets the limits for margin loans, and it's currently 50 percent—that is, your equity has to equal 50 percent of the total value of your account. So if you borrow $100,000, you must have at least $50,000 in your account that's your own. Otherwise, you'll get a margin call. You can still get into a great deal of trouble with a 50 percent margin loan, but not as much as you can at 10 percent or less. The marvelous thing about margin is that you can use it on most any type of investment—mortgage-backed securities, for example.

Bear Stearns pioneered a remarkable new structure for funding CDOs, called "Klio funding." As we mentioned earlier, the typical buyers for CDOs were institutional investors, such as pension funds and mutual funds. Klio funding allowed another type of investor to fund CDOs: Money market mutual funds.

Now, this may seem surprising to you, since money funds invest in very high-quality, short-term investments, such as Treasury bills or jumbo CDs. They do this to make sure that people can always redeem shares at $1 per share. For more than 30 years, people have treated money funds as high-yielding checking accounts, and, with almost no exceptions, their faith has been rewarded. Only one money fund, a tiny bank fund in Colorado, has ever redeemed shares for less than $1—"breaking a buck," as it's known in the industry.

Ralph Cioffi, a top hedge-fund manager at Bear Stearns, was the inventor of Klio funding. It worked like this. The Klios borrowed money by issuing short-term, high-quality IOUs, called commercial paper. They used the proceeds from their borrowings to buy long-term, high-yielding investments—such as, say, mortgages. The difference between the cost of borrowing and the interest from the mortgages was the funds' profits.

Money market funds won't buy just anyone's commercial paper, however. To make Klio funding suitable for money market funds, Citigroup guaranteed interest and principal. From a money fund's perspective, Klio commercial paper offered higher yields and good safety, since any default would land squarely on Citi's back.

The Klio model was such a success that other firms on Wall Street, notably Barclay's, Bank of America, and Society Generale, copied it.[10] All told, some $100 billion was funneled into these CDOs. As David Henry and Matthew Goldstein said in *Business Week:*

> The flood of fresh money (from money funds) made it even cheaper and easier for buyers to get mortgages. That, in turn, drove up home prices, holding off defaults and foreclosures. The process enriched the people who bought earlier in the boom and triggered more speculation.[11]

Arguably the worst timed and worst investment in the whole mortgage mania was the Bear Stearns High-Grade Credit Enhanced Leveraged Fund. This fund, sold to sophisticated investors, was leveraged up to its eyeballs. Investors had $600 million in the fund; it borrowed an additional six billion, making it leveraged by nearly 30 times. It made its debut in August, 2007. What could possibly go wrong?

Chapter 4

Matters Become
More Serious

A rlo Guthrie, in one of his talking blues songs, once noted that whenever you're feeling down, your friends will point at someone who's worse off than you are. "You think you have it bad?" your friends will ask. "Look at that guy!" And somehow, you will feel better, knowing that there's one guy in the world who has it worse than you do.

But there are a finite amount of people in the world, so somewhere, there must be a *last guy*: The one guy that's so low, so downtrodden, so unfortunate, that there's no one lower in the great chain of human misery.

Somewhere in the world, too, is the one person who bought the NASDAQ composite at 5,060.34, the very peak of the intraday peak. Someone, somewhere, bought gold at $850 an ounce, its 1980 peak. (It finally broke that level, 28 years later.) And, somewhere, someone paid the highest amount for a house in August 2006, which was when the U.S. housing bubble peaked.

Bubbles are marked, of course, by outrageous prices. Everyone laughs at how out of hand things have gotten, but prices will continue to rise as long as people believe that the fundamental premise behind the bubble is intact.

In 1999, for example, most market participants knew that the technology bubble was way, way overdone. There was a kind of giddy joy to it. A Super Bowl ad for e-trade, for example, featured a man being wheeled into a hospital. "Outta the way!" a medic yells. "This man has money coming out his wazoo!" The condition reversed itself, presumably, a few months later.

By late 2005, just about everyone knew that the housing market was overheated, but few seemed willing to call it a bubble. Yet only Robert Shiller and *The Economist*, a bastion of skepticism, were pushing hard for the housing market to be called a bubble.

On June 13, 2005, *Time* magazine published its "Home $weet Home" issue, featuring a cover on "Why we're going gaga over real estate." An interesting, and not always entirely trustworthy, market indicator is that whenever a business story hits the cover of a general-interest news magazine, the trend it observes has already peaked.

This is not to knock *Time* or *Newsweek*, which have some of the best business reporters in the business. But a major weekly news magazine has many stories competing for its cover: Politics, and wars and pop stars, among other things. And business, to most people, is boring. So when a business story rises to cover-story status, it's because top editors can no longer ignore the screaming of business reporters and editors, and concede that the trend might be worthy of a cover. By that time, of course, the trend has peaked and moved in the other direction.

In the late 1980s, Fidelity Investments, the gargantuan Boston-based mutual fund company, had a chart of the stock market from the 1800s. (It may still have.) At major turning points in the market, one of the analysts had pasted news magazine covers, which made a pretty convincing case for using them as contrary indicators. The covers were nearly always wrong.

Some very big hitters indeed were housing bubble skeptics. Federal Reserve Chairman Alan Greenspan, in a bit of understatement that would later haunt him, said in June 2005: "Although a 'bubble' in home prices for the nation as a whole does not appear likely, there do appear to be, at a minimum, signs of froth in some local markets where home prices seem to have risen to unsustainable levels." But he also said that there were natural barriers to wild-eyed real estate speculation, particularly when owners live in their houses. Greenspan noted that structural checks exist against rampant speculation in real estate, particularly when owners live in their houses.[1]

Ben Bernanke, now chairman of the Federal Reserve and then chairman of the President's Council of Economic Advisors, wasn't convinced there was a national housing bubble, either. "While speculative behavior has certainly surfaced in a few markets, it is important to keep in mind that there are also very strong economic fundamentals in play in the housing market," he said during a July, 2005 speech at the American Enterprise Institute.[2]

David Lereah, chief economist for the National Association of Realtors, was probably the biggest bubble denier. Lereah analyzed dozens of local housing markets and concluded, in his "anti-bubble reports," that there was no bubble in those markets or elsewhere. For the Washington, D.C. area, for example, the executive summary read:

> "With home prices rising strongly in most parts of the country, there has been widespread media coverage on the possibility of a housing market bust. A thorough analysis of the Washington-Arlington-Alexandria metro market, detailed below, reveals there is very little danger of this ..."[3]

Nevertheless, house prices had indeed peaked by the summer of 2006. The median price of a single-family home (half were higher, half lower) hit $230,900 in the third quarter of 2006, according to the National Association of Realtors. (See Figure 4.1.) Not surprisingly, the NAR's affordability index hit a multi-year low that month as well. By November, the

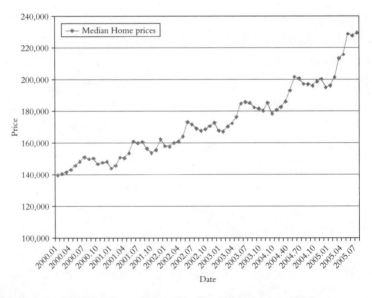

Figure 4.1 Median Home Prices January 2000–August 2005
Source: National Association of Realtors.

median price had slipped to $216,700. It rallied, briefly, but had plunged to $195,600 by the end of February 2008.

The Pin that Bursts the Bubble

What causes a bubble to stop expanding? Sometimes, there's an exogenous factor. The great Florida land bubble of the 1920s finally ended when a hurricane swept through Miami in 1926, literally washing some speculators out.

But the Florida land bubble started to go bust before that. When a bubble pops, it's pricked by a tiny speck of disbelief. Is a house with no basement really worth $500,000? Shouldn't you have more than two bathrooms in a $1 million home? Is any fixer-upper worth $1.5 million?

And, as if to confirm those suspicions, housing affordability, tracked by the National Association of Realtors, fell to its lowest level in 14 years in the last three months of 2005. The index baseline of 100 means that the average family can afford the median-priced home. As the line goes above 100, homes are more affordable; as the line goes below 100, homes are less affordable. Thus, by the realtor's lights, homes had gone from very affordable to affordable. One must bear in mind that to those who sell real estate, the glass is never half-empty: It's full. (See Figure 4.2.)

Even more importantly, mortgage payments were taking up a larger and larger percentage of peoples' incomes. A rule of thumb in mortgage lending is that you cannot afford your home if the payments are more than 30 percent of your pre-tax income. By that definition, 27 percent of all homeowners couldn't afford their homes in 2007. By 2006, 37 percent did.[4]

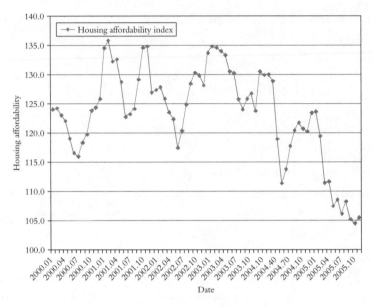

Figure 4.2   Housing affordability, 2000–2005
Source: National Association of Realtors.

As skepticism about real estate mounted, other, fundamental changes were starting to take place too. For one thing, interest rates were no longer falling. In fact, the Fed had started nudging its key short-term fed funds rate higher in 2004. By the start of 2006, the fed funds rate was 4.25 percent, up from 1 percent just two years earlier and on its way to 5.25 percent in June of that year.

And by raising the rate to 5.25 percent, the Fed wasn't trying to shut down the economy. It was really pushing monetary policy into neutral from a prolonged period of overdrive. After all, if another recession were to come, lowing interest rates from 1 percent to zero would not have much effect. If the Fed were ever going to lower rates again, it had to get to a reasonable altitude first.

Nevertheless, by raising rates, the Fed was signaling that they days of easy money were over. And it was also draining money out of the monetary system and making money less available—which is not particularly conducive to maintaining a housing bubble.

The fed funds rate isn't a prime mover of mortgage rates—mortgages tend to follow the 10-year Treasury bill yield instead. Those rates are set by the bond market, not the Fed.

Although the bond market isn't obligated to follow the Fed's lead, it did this time, reversing the trend in mortgage rates that had sparked the housing bubble in the first place. As a general rule of thumb, each 1 percentage point fall in interest rates adds another 300,000 to 400,000 new home buyers. When the bubble started in 2001, mortgage rates had averaged about 7 percent. By 2003, they had fallen to 5.23 percent, and housing prices soared.

But by July 2005, rates had crept back to 5.70 percent, and by 2006, mortgage rates averaged 6.41 percent. Suddenly, low rates were no longer creating a huge pool of buyers. Instead, higher rates were pushing new buyers out of the market.

At the same time that prices of existing homes were soaring and interest rates were rising, new homes were being built at a frenetic pace. Housing starts for single-family homes soared to a record 1.7 million in 2005, up from 1.2 million in 2000, according to the National Association of Home Builders. Those buyers who were left were not facing a shortage of homes any more: They had a plethora of choices. And there's no need to get into a bidding war for a house built 20 years ago, when there are 120 brand-new homes being built a mile away.

By the end of 2006, the glut of new houses, combined with higher interest rates and a shrinking pool of people eligible to buy, all but guaranteed at least a downturn. But another factor began to push up the supply of homes on the market—foreclosures.

The foreclosure boom started in 2006, but exploded in 2007. February 2007 saw 140,000 home foreclosures, according to Realtytrac. That jumped to nearly 180,000 in May and a staggering 240,000 in September. Many of these had been owned by speculators who were hoping to flip houses quickly, but found instead that the homes were worth less than when they bought them.

Typically, they bought the houses through no-doc or low-doc "liar's loans," which required little more than a signature and a credit check. Once they were under water, speculators had no compunctions about mailing the keys to the bank and walking away. Many other foreclosures were first-time homeowners whose adjustable-rate mortgage had reset to a higher, and unaffordable, rate.

The problem with foreclosures is that they drive prices down further. Banks do not like to own real estate. In fact, most hate it. They want to sell the house, recoup as much of their money as possible, and move on to the next lending disaster. Banks are the ultimate motivated seller: Not only do they want to get rid of the property, they can often afford to take a loss. When a foreclosure hits the market, it's not going to sell at a higher price than everything else on the block.

Even worse, when a foreclosed property gets sold at a bargain price in your neighborhood, everyone's home price falls. Real estate agents look at sales of comparable houses when they suggest a selling price for your home. If you own a $500,000 house and a similar house gets sold at auction for $400,000, suddenly your house is worth $400,000.

In Dallas, realtors were already noticing the huge supply of unsold new homes and foreclosed homes on the market. "The Metroplex has a glut of new homes sitting vacant, one of the highest mortgage delinquency rates in the country and a long run of rising foreclosures," Mitchell Schnurman wrote in February 2007 for the *Fort Worth Star-Telegram*. "Taken together, the trends point to the most ominous local housing market since the real-estate bust of 1986."[5]

Sales weren't going too well on Pickett Lane in Herndon, Virginia, either. We might recall that in 2005, 408 Pickett Lane sold for $400,000, about $118,000 more than the county had assessed it for tax purposes. In June, 2007, the house reverted to bank ownership at a listed price of $390,000—presumably, the amount of the mortgage note.

Other houses in the neighborhood were having troubles, too. 417 Pickett Lane, which had sold for $445,000 in December 2005, changed hands in September 2007, but not voluntarily: The Bank of New York assumed ownership for $389,000. A third home on the block, reverted to the Federal Home Loan Mortgage Corp. In the space of a year, three of 18 homes on the block, or 17 percent, were owned by the bank.

Pickett Lane wasn't the only neighborhood enveloped in foreclosures, nor was it the worst, by any stretch of the imagination. In Aurora, Illinois, foreclosures jumped 50 percent in 2007 from 2006.[6] In Las Vegas, 1 out of every 150 households were in foreclosure. In Detroit, the ratio hit 1 in 29 in August, 2007; in Stockton, California, it was 1 in 27.

Default Comes to Wall Street

We talked in Chapter 3 about the risks of leverage. A mortgage loan is one simple use of leverage: A borrower uses big amounts of someone else's money to buy a very large asset. During the subprime meltdown, homeowners and investors alike discovered just how dangerous leverage could be. If you buy a house for nothing down and the price falls, you have to write a check to the bank to sell it. It took Wall Street to take that level of danger to an entirely new level.

Until the mortgage crisis, mortgages were pretty dull investments. Default rates for prime loans—those loans that honestly conformed to Freddie Mac and Fannie Mae lending standards—were often less than 1 percent. People who have invested their life savings in a dream home are likely to do anything they can to avoid default. And Freddie Mac and Fannie Mae, you will recall, guaranteed timely principal and interest payments of the mortgages in their mortgage-backed securities.

Even subprime defaults tended to be fairly low—about 5 to 7 percent of all subprime loans, under normal conditions— which is why they seemed so appealing to Wall Street. Investors could earn rates well above comparable Treasury bonds, but without as much risk as, say, bonds issued by corporations of dubious credit quality.

When investment banks started to package subprime loans into securities, as you may recall, they sliced those securities into different sub-packages, called "tranches." The top tranche would get the lowest interest rate, but wouldn't have to worry about defaults until they reached an unimaginably high level— say, 20 percent or more. The next tranche would get a higher rate, but have more exposure to defaults. The bottom tranche would get the highest rate of all, but it would have to eat the first 10 percent or so of bad mortgage paper.

Mortgage packagers, as part of their underwriting duties, would run computer simulations on the packages to see what the effect of unimaginably high default rates would be. At the time, those default rates would be, perhaps, 10 to 12 percent. The results were not pretty, but the top tranches would be fairly safe. The bottom tranches? Well, those were sold to sophisticated investors, who presumably knew the risks they were taking. And, in 2005 and early 2006, subprime mortgage-backed securities seemed like a good way for a money manager to goose returns with what seemed like relatively little risk. After all, the economy was strong, interest rates were low, and the housing markets were humming. Hedge funds and even a few mutual funds bought them and collected big yields, making shareholders happy.

What no one on Wall Street had counted on was the magnitude of the wave of defaults that began in 2007 as buyers deserted the real estate market and interest rates began to creep up. By the second quarter of 2007:

- 14.8 percent of all subprime loans were delinquent.
- 5.5 percent were in foreclosure.
- 8.0 percent of all adjustable-rate subprime loans were in foreclosure, and 17 percent were delinquent.

Those are just averages. In many areas, the situation was worse. Let's consider Iowa, not usually considered a land of bug-eyed speculation. In the second quarter of 2007, 8.63 percent of all subprime loans in Iowa were in foreclosures, the fourth-highest in the country. A staggering 13.7 percent of all Iowa subprime ARMs were in foreclosure.[7] Subprime default rates were at recession levels—even though the economy was still robust.

Typically, a mortgage default doesn't mean a total loss for the lender. The bank, after all, owns the property, which it can resell to recoup some or all of its losses. This works fine when the property is sensibly valued when the bank makes the loan. When the property is valued at sky-high bubble prices? Not so much.

Rather than more typical 70 to 80 percent recoveries on defaults, banks were recovering about 50 percent of the amount loaned—and that's not including the costs of the foreclosure process, which can be considerable. After all, you have to send myriad threatening letters to the mortgage holder, evict them, secure the property, and maintain it while you wait for it to be sold.

The first casualties—at least in the business world—were the subprime lenders. They were overwhelmed, in part, by defaults. More seriously, however, they could no longer sell their loans to Wall Street and get money to make more subprime loans. In March, 2007, New Century Financial, one of the largest subprime lenders, announced that it would stop lending. It filed for bankruptcy protection on April 2. It was the largest of 25 subprime lenders that failed in the first four months of the year.

Existing home sales fell 8.4 percent in April 2007, the largest drop in 18 years—and particularly shocking because April is normally the kindest month for home sales. People like to shop for homes in the springtime, so they can get settled into their new house in time for school to begin in September. Normally, springtime means a thriving business in real estate. This year, however, buyers decided to wait.

In the meantime, those who had invested in packages of subprime mortgages discovered, to their horror, what happens when your computer models don't quite reflect the worst that could happen. If you owned one of the lower-rated tranches, for example, you had two problems. The first was that defaults reduced your principal. For example, if you bought $10 million of subprime-backed securities and 10 percent defaulted, your securities would be worth $9 million.

But nothing on Wall Street is bought or sold because of its current price. People buy stocks and bonds based on what they think their future values will be. And, as buyers of mortgage-backed securities peered into the future, all they could see were more defaults coming. So if you wanted to sell your mortgage-backed securities, you had to make concessions not only for those loans that had defaulted, but for the buyers' worst fears of future defaults.

Discounts of 35 percent or more were common for many of the lower subprime tranches, and, as default rates ratcheted higher, mid-level and even upper-level tranches were dinged, too. This could be particularly difficult for money managers, because they had to tell shareholders what the current value of their securities were. Let's say, for example, that you held the $10 million mortgage-backed security that had had 10 percent of the pool default.

You couldn't claim a $9 million asset. Instead, you had to mark your securities to market—that is, report their value according to their current market value. Because mortgage-backed securities are not traded very often, you could use computer models to estimate the value of the bond or you could use a pricing service, whose job is to estimate the value of your bond. Imagine, then, the surprise of managers when the estimated value of their $10 million in mortgage-backed securities came in at $7 million, $6.5 million, even $6 million.

For hedge-fund shareholders, the news was even worse: If a fund's holdings are valued at a 35 percent discount, that's the price shareholders get for their shares, even if management has no plan to sell the offending investments.

And if management didn't plan to sell those securities, that was probably a good thing, because they probably couldn't find anyone to buy them. Unlike stocks, mortgage-backed securities aren't traded on an exchange. Instead, they are traded between large institutions in an informal network of dealers. If you have a large block of mortgage-backed securities to sell, you start making phone calls and getting bids. Bond dealers, for all their high-tech equipment, rely as much on a telephone and a phone list as they do on their computer screens.

Suddenly, the voices on the other end of the line were no longer quite so friendly. The ocean of liquidity that had buoyed the housing bubble was suddenly a desert. Trading fell to nothing. Even if you slashed your mortgage-backed security's price, you probably couldn't find a buyer. Could matters possibly get any worse? Of course they could.

Death of a Hedge Fund

Civil war buffs like to argue about the point at which the South lost the war. Some say it was at Appomattox, where Grant and Lee signed the terms of surrender for the Army of Northern Virginia. Others say it was at Gettysburg, where the South lost its most crucial battle. Still others say the South lost the war when the first shot was fired at Ft. Sumter, because the Confederacy had neither the arms nor the men to beat the Union in the first place.

Similarly, people will probably debate when Bear Stearns' course became fatal. It may have been when it entered the subprime mortgage business. But a good place to start would probably be the death of its two hedge funds in June 2007.

A hedge fund is a freewheeling investment pool for the very wealthy. Because it has a limited number of investors, and because those investors are sophisticated (and rich), hedge funds are fairly lightly regulated. Unlike mutual funds, for example, hedge funds can use vast amounts of leverage and move between all different types of markets, from currencies to bonds to stocks and back.

Hedge-fund managers can use all kinds of strategies that, in the right hands, work quite well. In the wrong hands, they could blow a portfolio into flinders. In money management, as with building demolition, execution is everything.

Hedge funds had garnered a great deal of attention—and money—because some very prominent hedge-fund managers had made a great deal of money for investors. George Soros, for example, made a fortune on his hedge fund, as did John Henry, the current owner of the Red Sox. (Many others had closed their doors, never to be heard from again, but Wall Street tended to ignore that.)

The lovely thing about hedge funds, from a manager's point of view, is how lucrative they are for the manager. Management charges 2 percent of the money invested in the pool, whether it makes money or not. It also takes 20 percent of the profit, an arrangement called a "two-and-twenty" deal.

A manager of a $250 million hedge fund, which is considered small in the mutual fund world, could make far more money running the hedge fund than he could in the mutual fund industry. He would take home $5 million as the base fee of 2 percent of the fund's assets. If the hedge fund earned a gross profit of 20 percent, he would get an additional $10 million. A mutual fund manager running the same amount of money would be lucky to get $1 million.

Astonishingly, sophisticated investors think that giving away all that money to the manager is a good deal. Many even pay additional fees to advisors, who tell them which hedge funds are the best.

Bear Stearns, which had emerged as one of the biggest players in the mortgage-backed securities markets, offered two hedge funds that invested in mortgage-backed securities. But you can invest in mortgage-backed securities most anywhere for fairly little. Vanguard, for example, offers a fund of ultra safe GNMA securities for just $21 a year for every $10,000 invested.

To goose the returns from the Bear Stearns funds, management invested in subprime mortgages and used leverage to buy them. As in any margin agreement, the funds used their holdings as collateral for loans. They then used the borrowed money to buy more mortgage-backed securities. All of this worked quite well until the value of mortgage-backed securities started to plunge.

As the funds started to lose money, they started getting margin calls from their creditors—the banks and investment banks that had loaned them money to buy mortgage-backed securities. The funds' creditors wanted Bear to either put up

more collateral—or to sell enough to satisfy the loan agreements. To meet the margin calls, the Bear funds had to sell their
mortgage-backed securities. Unfortunately, because the market
for mortgage-backed securities was so thin, they couldn't raise
enough money to meet their creditors' demands. So their creditors seized the loan collateral.

The result, as Bear, Stearns told investors in a "Dear client"
letter in July 2007, was utter catastrophe. The most leveraged
fund, called the "enhanced fund," had had $638 million in capi-
tal on March 1. It now had nothing left. The other fund, which
once had had $950 million in capital, now had about 9 percent
of its assets left, the letter explained. The funds filed for bankruptcy on August 1.

About this time, the subprime crisis went from being a
slow-moving train wreck to a very quick one indeed. Quite
simply, no one wanted to buy subprime mortgages, and nobody
wanted to lend to subprime lenders.

On August 6, American Home Mortgage, once the nation's
tenth-largest mortgage lender, declared bankruptcy. More omi-
nously, the list of its biggest creditors was a *Who's Who* of Wall
Street banking houses. At the same time, two other big lenders,
National City and Aegis Mortgage, stopped taking loan applications—generally a death rattle for a mortgage lender.

After American Home Mortgage collapsed in just 10 days,
all eyes were on Countrywide Mortgage, which had issued
about 17 percent of all mortgages in the U.S. On Thursday,
August 16, Countrywide announced that it had to tap its $11.5
billion credit line. Having a bank tap a gargantuan credit line
is a bit like having a doctor bolt out of the room after exam-
ining a patient. It's not a calming thing. And, in fact, the very

next day, many of Countrywide's depositors decided that another bank would be a better place to have their checking accounts.

On August 17th, the Federal Reserve, normally noted for the stately, measured pace of their actions, slashed the discount rate by half a percentage point. In addition, the Fed said it would accept mortgage-backed securities as collateral for repurchase agreements.

These two actions are important. The discount window is where banks get loans from the Fed. The catch is this: If you're a bank and you need a loan from the Fed, it means no one else will give you a loan. The Fed is the lender of last resort. As you might suspect, bellying up to the discount window is *not done*, unless the situation is particularly dire.

The second action is a bit arcane, but also quite important. A repurchase agreement works like this. Bank A needs an overnight loan. So it agrees to sell securities to Bank B and then buy them back the next day, at a slightly higher price. The higher price is Bank B's interest.

What's nice about repurchase agreements from a lender's point of view, is that it's fully collateralized. If Bank A shuffles off to oblivion the next day, Bank B still has Bank A's securities. (Discount window loans, too, are collateralized.)

But when the Fed agreed to take mortgage-backed securities as collateral for repurchase agreements, it gave some banks important breathing room. The Fed was taking temporarily illiquid securities—mortgage-backed securities—and giving out cash. A bank with a big portfolio of locked-up mortgages could, in effect, become liquid again.

To some extent, the move reflected Fed chairman Ben Bernanke's long study of the Depression and the governmental tactics used to get the nation's financial system going again. Although it didn't go as far as buying loans outright from banks, it was an innovative step to make banks liquid again— and in the ensuing disaster, liquidity was the difference between failure and survival, as Bear Stearns would find out.

Nevertheless, the subprime crisis continued to gather steam—and victims. On August 31, Ameriquest closed its doors. Ameriquest was a financial powerhouse through much of the decade, sponsoring Rolling Stones tours as well as the Texas Rangers' baseball field. (Free stock advice: Never, ever, invest in a company that has a sports stadium named after it.) The company's CEO, Roland Arnall, was named U.S. ambassador to the Netherlands.[8]

That same day, President Bush announced a plan to help homeowners who had fallen behind on subprime loans. One move allowed subprime borrowers who were still in their homes to refinance, under certain conditions. Another temporarily removed a dreadful tax rule. Under the law, if a lender forgave part of a mortgage loan during the workout process, that portion was considered taxable income to the borrower. In other words, if the bank forgave you $30,000 on a home loan, that $30,000 was added to your income at tax time.

Bad news continued. In September, Northern Rock, a British bank, had an old-fashioned run on the bank, as thousands of depositors scrambled to get their money from the bank before a rumored collapse. Merrill Lynch recorded a $5.5 billion loss in October.

Throughout the fall, both the Fed and the President worked feverishly to calm the subprime crisis, as it quickly became known in the press. The Fed dropped the fed funds rate from 5.25 percent at the start of 2007 to 4.75 percent in September and 4.25 percent by the end of the year.

President Bush announced the formation of the Hope Now Alliance, an alliance between the government and private lenders to help subprime homeowners. Although the Alliance was often ineffectual—lenders rarely gave much help—some lenders did announce a freeze on adjustable-rate mortgage payment hikes in December.

Nevertheless, the news from the financial sector was unrelentingly awful. Earnings season, for Wall Street, became confession season. In October, Citigroup, the nation's largest bank, wrote down $2.2 billion of subprime loans from its books. In November, Merrill Lynch stunned the financial community with a $7.9 billion write down.

Meanwhile, at Bear Stearns . . .

Bear Stearns, as you may recall, made its name in mortgage-backed securities. By August, 2007, that was no longer a good thing.

Bear had reported that its profits were down 10 percent in the second quarter of 2007, but it was hardly alone in getting clobbered. Most financial services stocks were getting hit hard too. In September, however, it revealed a truly shocking quarterly report: Profits were down 61 percent from the already awful second quarter. In an effort to calm its creditors, CEO James Cayne said, "Most of our businesses are beginning to rebound."

Of course, this is what CEOs are paid to do. Whenever something really dreadful happens, it's the CEO's job to stand up, look deeply into the camera, and say things he probably doesn't mean. In December, the news got worse: Bear was forced to write down $1.5 billion in assets, and announced its first-ever quarterly loss.

The next day, PIMCO, the West Coast bond giant, decided to unwind some of its trades with Bear Stearns. Although Bear was able to postpone the break off, it was a body blow to the company's reputation.

Cayne, who had spent much of the time during the meltdown of his hedge funds playing bridge in Chicago, had missed several opportunities to partner with other companies, most notably Kohlberg, Kravis & Roberts, the legendary takeover house. (Henry Kravis was a Bear Stearns alumni, as were the other founders of KKR). By January, he was out, replaced by Bear veteran Alan Schwartz.

Schwartz had a brief period—until about March—of respite. Then, rumors started swirling around Wall Street that Bear Stearns was running low on cash and running short of friends who would lend them more.

In fact, Bear Stearns had plenty of cash: Some $18 billion or so at the start of its last week. But the rumors proved more powerful than its cash. Bear's business partners worried about counterparty risk, a broad term meaning, basically, the deep-seated fear that Bear wouldn't be able to live up to its trading agreements. And those trading agreements were many and varied. Companies relied on Bear to buy or sell large blocks of securities: If Bear folded in mid-transaction, the counterparty could be left with millions of dollars in limbo.

One by one, in rapid succession, they shifted their trading to competitors.

Even worse, the companies that Bear Stearns could normally count on for short-term loans didn't want to do business with Bear either. Typically, an investment bank not only keeps billions of dollars of cash on hand, but also arranges credit lines for temporary shortfalls. Alarmed by the rumors surrounding Bear, these lenders, too, turned their backs.

By Thursday, March 13, Bear Stearns had ripped through $15 billion of its own cash, and clients were still fleeing. No one would lend it money to continue operations. Schwartz, seeing the writing on the wall, called James Dimon, CEO of JPMorgan Chase, to ask about a merger.

At the same time, the Federal Reserve was getting worried, too. It knew that a collapse of Bear Stearns could create a collapse in the money market—the network of overnight loans that kept the nation's businesses running. Already, bets on Bear's collapse were mounting, in the form of default insurance on its bonds. Like the premiums for a driver with five moving violations, the premiums to insure Bear's bonds against default were soaring.

The Fed, too, was worried what would happen if Bear collapsed, leaving billions of dollars in contracts frozen in legal proceedings. By Friday, Fed officials were in the Bear Stearns offices, trying to figure out what to do.

The solution: A 28-day line of credit, arranged via JPMorgan Chase. But JPM would be just the conduit: The Fed would be the lender. By law, the Fed doesn't lend to investment banks. JPMorgan Chase, however, was a commercial bank, and the Fed could lend to them. So the loan was funneled through

JPMorgan Chase, marking the first time in history that the Fed had acted to bail out an investment bank.

But Wall Street was not reassured. Clients continued to leave Bear Stearns, the stock collapsed, and the Fed became increasingly concerned. On Friday afternoon, Schwartz got a call from both the Secretary of the Treasury and the president of the New York Federal Reserve Bank, Timothy Geithner. Their message: Time was up. Bear needed to have a buyer by Monday.[9]

After a weekend of tense negotiating, the offer was on the table: $2 a share for Bear Stearns, which had sold for $172 a share in January 2007. The Fed would lend $10 billion to JPMorgan Chase, which would assume the first $1 billion of losses from Bear's illiquid mortgage-backed securities. Bear Stearns accepted the offer, which was later sweetened to $10 a share.

The subprime crisis did not end with the collapse of Bear Stearns. At this writing, it's still going on. Lehman Brothers posted a $2.8 billion loss in June. AIG, the global insurance giant, ousted its CEO after posting its two largest quarterly losses in history.

Chapter 5

Where Do We Go from Here?

A minute before noon on Friday, May 30, JPMorgan Chase & Co., completed the acquisition of Bear Stearns. Shareholders at Bear Stearns got 0.21753 shares of JPMorgan Chase. Based on JPM's closing price of $43 per share, each Bear Stearns share was finally valued at $9.35. After 85 years, Bear Stearns passed into history.

Ironically, Bear Stearns memorabilia sold for more than the stock itself. A day later on eBay, the online auction house, you could buy a Bear Stearns promotional hard hat with the slogan "Repackaging risk" for $49. A Bear Stearns teddy bear—in suit and tie—was selling for $24.99. The owner of a Bear Stearns Asset Management beach towel was asking $15.99.

Naturally, you could also buy a t-shirt that says, "I invested my life savings in Bear Stearns, and all I have left is this lousy T-shirt."

So, what can an investor learn from all this? Possibly the most succinct explanation comes from Kurt Vonnegut, author of *Slaughterhouse Five* and *The Sirens of Titan*. In one of his lesser novels, *Slapstick,* Vonnegut observed: "History is merely a list of surprises. It can only prepare us to be surprised again."

And, indeed, most of financial history is a list of surprises. Many great inventions have been ignored for decades before someone finds a surprising use for them. The Romans, for example, had toys that spun around on steam power, yet never created a steam-powered chariot. (They would have loved NASCAR). Thomas Edison, no slouch in business and marketing, thought the main application for the phonograph would be as an office dictating tool. Thomas Watson, founder of IBM, once said that there was a world market for perhaps five computers.

Similarly, we're almost always surprised when an investment trend changes. A decade ago, for example, a case of Budweiser cost more than a 42-gallon barrel of oil. Back then, the biggest fear was that members of the Organization of Petroleum Exporting Countries, the oil cartel, would break ranks, compete furiously to produce oil, and drive prices down more. Under that scenario, "there's nowhere to go but down," said Gordon Platt, then financial editor of the highly respected *Journal of Commerce*.[1]

If we go back another decade, to 1988, the last thing anyone would have expected was the collapse of the Soviet Union, the reunification of Germany, and the emergence of a single, powerful European currency, the Euro. It was the kind of prediction you'd expect to read in the late, lamented *Weekly World News*, along with stories about skeletons found floating in the

Atlantic with *Titanic* life jackets. We tend to assume that whatever is happening now will happen forever.

And, shortly after big, world-changing surprises, you always hear people claim that they knew all along that these things would happen. In most cases, they are either not telling the truth, or they were off fairly substantially on their timing—which is the same as being wrong. In 2008, for example, the price of an ounce of gold soared to about $1,000 for the first time in history, and many longtime gold bugs were ecstatic: Hadn't they, after all, predicted it?

Well, sure. But they predicted $1,000-an-ounce gold back in 1981, when gold spiked, briefly, to $850 an ounce. And in investing, too soon is too bad. Had you bought at $850 an ounce and sold at $1,000, you would have earned $150 in 27 years—less than 1 percent a year. (Many of those who predicted $1,000 gold in 1980, incidentally, actually saw $1,000 as a step on the way to even loftier levels. The Aden sisters, Mary Ann and Pamela, predicted $3,000 gold.)

And so it goes. In the financial world, there are bad surprises, like the collapse of Bear Stearns, and good ones, like the Euro. The Securities and Exchange Commission, which is not noted for their sparkling writing, has a succinct phrase that says, essentially, what Vonnegut says: Past performance is no guarantee of future returns. How, then, do you prepare for surprises?

The answer, quite simply, is that you spread your investment net wide enough that some part of it will respond well to most emergencies. There are several important caveats to this advice, and we'll cover them all. But the first is this: You shouldn't be so terrified of all the awful possibilities in the world that you don't invest, or that you invest inappropriately.

You have to invest because, ultimately, the greatest danger to your money is inflation. We're not talking hyperinflation here, where a wheelbarrow of bills won't buy you a loaf of bread. We're talking everyday, low-level inflation. Let's say that you save $100,000 and stuff it in your mattress. You buy a dog to guard the mattress, and a gun so you can guard the dog. After 10 years of 3 percent inflation, your $100,000 will have the buying power of $73,742. After 20 years, its value will shrink to $54,000.

So if you do nothing with your money, you will lose it. It's the Red Queen effect, named after the Red Queen in Alice in Wonderland. In the book, Alice and the Red Queen are running a race, but not moving.

> "Well, in our country," said Alice, still panting a little, "you'd generally get to somewhere else—if you run very fast for a long time, as we've been doing."
>
> "A slow sort of country!" said the Queen. "Now, here, you see, it takes all the running you can do, to keep in the same place. If you want to get somewhere else, you must run at least twice as fast as that!"[2]

If you want your savings to beat inflation, you have to stay invested just to make sure it maintains its purchasing power. So even if you're sure that the country is going to slide into the next Great Depression, you shouldn't be paralyzed by terror. You need to invest.

As unknowable as the future is you still must at least start with a plan. Making a plan doesn't mean that you can never swerve from it, or that you can't alter it as events changes—in fact, that's what most intelligent investors do. John Maynard Keynes, one of the most brilliant economists and investors of the 20th century, was once chided for changing his position on monetary policy during the Great Depression. His response: "When facts change, I change my mind. What do you do, sir?"

Financial planning brings to mind oak-paneled rooms and expensive people in expensive suits charging expensive fees. But even if you do go to a high-end financial planner, you'll go through this same exercise. So why not try it for free, first?

Making a Wish

We're constantly admonished not to throw money at problems, but as Vonnegut noted, that's what money is *for*. (We'll stop with the Vonnegut quotes here.) You use money to solve problems like "How will I live when I retire? How will I get Johnny through college? When will I get to see Rome?"

But the first step in financial planning is to make a wish list and set some goals. What things would you like to do if you had the money? You should be realistic—living next door to Scarlett Johannsen or George Clooney is probably not in the cards. On the other hand, if you really want to own your own airplane or move to Pago-Pago with your college sweetheart, put that down, too. Your list might look like this:

- Put Johnny through college
- Retire to West Virginia
- Buy a hybrid Toyota
- Go to Argentina
- Get an electric guitar and learn how to play

Lists like these are best put in a drawer for a week and then looked at once again with fresh eyes. (Incidentally, if you're married or otherwise attached, making a list like this without the other party is utterly futile, or grounds for divorce, depending on the degree of your spouse's rage. If you're married, don't do this alone.)

Your next step: Put a date beside each goal.

- Put Johnny through college: 2020
- Retire to West Virginia: 2028
- Buy a hybrid Toyota: 2010
- Go to Argentina: 2009
- Get an electric guitar and learn how to play: 2028

Next, unfortunately, you have to put a price on all these things. Think of it as a reality check. Let's start with the Big One: Retirement. Most people would like to stop working and spend their golden years doing things they have always wanted to do. Make a garden. Climb the pyramids. Finish that creature in the basement.

You can figure your retirement needs in two ways: The quick way or the slow way.

The Quick Way

Assume you'll need about as much money when you retire as you are living on now. If you make $50,000 a year now, it would be nice to have $50,000 a year when you retire.

Financial planners tell you that you can get by on 70 percent of what your pre-retirement income, but that's increasingly looking like hogwash. People nowadays are healthier than their parents were when they retired. Today's retirees like to go out to dinner and travel, both of which will more than make up for any money saved from commuting. It's probably better to assume you'll spend about as much in retirement as you do now.

Unless you have reason to believe otherwise—a debilitating illness, for example, or a hobby that entails alcohol and explosives—you should assume that you'll live at least 20 years into retirement, and probably 30. The average woman now aged 65 lives to be 86.8 years. The average 65-year-old man lives to be about 81. But that's the average; half live longer. All things being equal, it's better for your money to outlast you than for you to outlast your money.

Planners typically recommend that your starting withdrawal be 4 to 5 percent of your retirement savings. Here's how to determine, in a back-of-the-envelope way, how much savings that translates into:

1. Determine the amount of money you'll need in a year. We'll say $50,000.
2. Divide that by the initial percentage you'll take out. We'll say 4 percent. So you divide $50,000 by 4 percent.
3. The answer? $1.25 million.

The Slow Way

Figure out your likely expenses in retirement, and aim for that. This is a more accurate figure, and a more useful approach if retirement is fast approaching. After all, you won't have to contribute 8 percent of your salary to a 401(k) plan for your retirement. Your taxes may be lower. If you plan to have a paid-up home, then you won't have to worry about mortgage payments, either.

If you're a real alpha geek, you can do this on an Excel spreadsheet, or in machine code, for that matter. Fortunately, there are lots of alpha geeks in the world who have some decent calculators. Many mutual fund companies do, for example. T. Rowe Price has a very good, simple worksheet on figuring out your retirement needs. For example, suppose you're 35, and you earn $50,000 a year. Using the assumptions in the worksheet (3 percent inflation, 25 percent tax rate, 8 percent investment growth, 90 percent income replacement, 7 percent earnings after you retire, no current savings), you'll need to have roughly $2 million when you retire.

These are daunting figures, and you should be aware that there's an assumption in them that makes them particularly daunting. Once again, it's the Red Queen effect: Even modest inflation means that you'll have to increase your withdrawals periodically to keep your standard of living. Those higher withdrawals will eventually overwhelm your earnings.

Now, there's no law saying that your withdrawals each year must be adjusted upwards for the current rate of inflation. A recent study shows that you can boost your withdrawals to 6 percent or so if you refrain from increasing your withdrawals in years when the stock market is down. So consider the numbers that you get as noble goals, rather than absolute necessities.

Don't forget that you may also have certain assets that will help you through. The biggest is your own personal earning power: It will be, ultimately, the source of nearly all your wealth. Despite the fact that raises at most companies have been tiny—typically in the 2 to 3 percent range—they may not stay that way forever. And if you get a new job, or move up a notch in management, your income could go up considerably, enabling you to save more. Other assets to consider:

Social Security. You may have heard the old saw that more people believe that they will see UFOs before they see a cent from Social Security. Great story! But it's not true. The Employee Benefit Research Institute, a remarkably sober and nonpartisan think tank, actually conducted a survey on the topic. The results: just 26 percent said it was more likely that aliens exist in space than it was that they would get Social Security.[3]

And, since most of Social Security is paid from payroll tax, EBRI says, you'd have to believe that Congress would repeal the Social Security payroll tax—something that's far less likely than aliens playing cricket on the White House lawn. Even if Congress does nothing to shore up Social Security, the system will continue to pay full benefits until 2042, at which point you will still get 73 percent of your benefits.

You can get an estimate of how much you will receive from Social Security at www.socialsecurity.gov. Click on "calculate your benefits."

Pensions. Traditional pensions, where you get a monthly check from your company, are on the decline. But many union and government jobs still offer them—and they are a valuable benefit. To get generate $1,000 a month for 30 years, you would need to deposit $175,000 in the bank and earn 5 percent on your money.

Your 401(k) plan. These self-directed retirement plans let you sock away money and not pay taxes on your earnings until you withdraw them at retirement. Any money you put

into a 401(k) is, of course, yours. If your company matches your contributions, those contributions become yours once you've satisfied your company's vesting requirements.
Good old Uncle Fred. Hey, you never know.

As you put prices on your wish list, you may find that you have to make some adjustments. It might be better, for example, to buy the car a year later, or to retire at 62 rather than 60. (Actually, that's a great idea, because Social Security may not kick in for you until then.) On the other hand, you might find that you can achieve some goals earlier: A good guitar doesn't cost that much, and, rather than building a soundproof bunker in the backyard, you could practice while everyone else is at the movies.

A Word about Risk

When you make investment decisions, you're actually making decisions about risk. Although financial experts have many different classifications of risk, for the average person, the basic measure of risk is this: How much money do I stand to lose?

Let's start with a simple benchmark: The yield on the 10-year Treasury note. A T-note is an IOU from the U.S. government, and, whatever you may think of our national debt, the government has the best credit rating on the planet. In theory, a T-note would be repaid before any other obligation of the government, including federal bank insurance. If you buy and hold a 10-year T-note, you'll collect regular interest and, at the end of the 10 years, get your principal back. As long as you hold it to maturity, it's a risk-free investment.

At this writing, a 10-year T-note yields 4.06 percent. (You can find the 10-year T-note yield in a variety of places, from Yahoo! Finance to *USA Today*'s Money section. So, at this writing, you can earn 4.06 percent for a decade with no risk.

That's not much. A $100,000 investment in a 10-year T-note will pay you just $4,060 a year. (That's $338 a month, for the morbidly curious. At that rate, you will double your money in 18 years.) If you want to earn more money, you will have to take more risk.

You could, for example, buy a top-rated bond from a large bank. At the moment, those yield 5.66 percent. Now, the odds of Citibank or Bank of America going down the tubes are relatively low, but not out of the realm of possibility. And for that bit of risk, you earn an extra 1.6 percentage points.

If you want to earn more than 5.66 percent, you have to take yet more risk. You could, for example, invest in high-yield, high-risk junk bonds, which are IOUs from companies with shaky credit ratings. They often return 10 percent or more, which means you could double your money in about seven years. That's the good news.

The bad news: Seven years after issuance, 18 to 26 percent of the bonds have defaulted, leaving investors with very expensive wallpaper.

Similarly, you could invest in the stock market. Your odds of beating the returns from a Treasury bill are good, but bear in mind that we're talking odds here, not certainties. Had you invested in the Standard & Poor's 500 stock index on January 1, 1999, you would have earned 21.04 percent on your money by Dec. 31, 1999. Had you invested on January 1, 2002, you would have lost 22.10 percent. You're taking real risk here.

The rule that risk increases with rewards has its limits, of course. Some risks just aren't worth taking. For example, a lottery ticket, in theory, could turn $1 into $30 million overnight. But the risk of losing your money is so high that it's just not worth it.

Match Your Investments with Your Goals

Most people like the idea of taking no risk, but loathe the idea of a 4.06 percent return. And there are several ways you can goose your returns without dreaming of dollar bills with wings flying away from you each night. But if you match your investments with your goals, you can reduce your risks and budget your goals at the same time.

Time is really your most important consideration. For example, stocks are a long-term investment, because they are too volatile on a year-to-year basis.

From April 1978 through April 2008, the S&P 500's worst 12-month period has been a 26.6 percent loss in 2001, according to Morningstar, which tracks investments of all types. The S&P 500's best period: a 61 percent gain in 1983.

But time soothes some of the pain.

- Worst 5-year period: -17 percent, for the period ended March 2003.
- Worst 10-year period: a gain of 41 percent, for the period ended March 2008.

For a very long period of time, stocks have produced the best overall returns. Ibbotson and Associates, a Chicago research firm, notes that large-company stocks have returned an average 10.25 percent a year since 1926, vs. 5.45 percent for U.S. government bonds and 3.73 percent for a three-month Treasury bill.

We do not know what the future holds. Even as you turn this page, the economy could be grinding to a dead halt. Nevertheless, we do know that over long periods of time, the stock market typically recovers from nasty, ugly periods, and still performs better than bonds or bank CDs. So if you have a long-term goal—say, a retirement that's a comfortable 10 or more years away—then it makes sense to have a large chunk of your portfolio in stocks. And in subsequent chapters, we'll talk about how to hedge your portfolio against big economic uglies.

If you diversify across a wide range of stocks from different industries, you'll increase your margin of safety, too. Although you'll lose some of the wild gains that you can get from individual stocks, you'll also lose some of the huge losses if you invest in a diversified portfolio of equities. Consider this:

Had you invested $1,000 in Bear Stearns on May 30, 2007, you would have had $62 left on May 30, 2008. But let's suppose, instead, that you had invested in a basket of financial services stocks. The Financial Select SPDR fund does precisely that. Because it's diversified, any losses from Bear Stearns would be shielded, a bit, by smaller losses—or even gains—in its other holdings. Your $1,000 would be at $740.30 over the same 12-month period. But let's say, instead, that you bought a fund that mirrored the S&P 500, which tracks the performance of large, financially strong companies. Your $1,000 would be worth $950.50.

Bonds Add Income and Safety

Bonds are long-term IOUs issued by the government, corporations, or municipal entities, such as states, counties, toll roads, and universities.

Bonds have two components: Income and principal. Let's start with income, and for that we'll use the U.S. Treasury's 30-year bond, which matures in February, 2038.

Because a bond is a loan, it carries a fixed interest rate, called the coupon rate. The term dates back to the 19th century, when bond certificates actually came with paper coupons around the side. To collect your interest, you snipped out a coupon and sent it to the issuer, which then sent you your interest payment.

The U.S. Treasury bond in our example has a coupon rate of 4.375 percent. If you own a $1,000 bond, the government will send you $43.75 a year. In February, 2038, the government will redeem your bond and return your $1,000. If you hold the bond to maturity, you'll get your interest and principal.

You can, however, buy and sell bonds. Let's say that in 2015 you decide to sell your bond. But in the past few years, interest rates have risen, and newly issued T-bonds yield 6 percent. Your bond, with its 4.375 percent yield, won't look very attractive to a buyer.

You can't go back to the Treasury and ask for a higher interest rate. A deal, after all, is a deal. But you could cut the bond's price. That way, the bond's yield—interest payment divided by price—would rise.

For example, if you slashed your bond's price to $725, its yield would rise to about 6 percent. ($43.75 divided by $725 is about 6 percent). So when interest rates rise, bond prices fall.

The reverse is also true: When rates fall, bond prices fall. Let's say that in 2015, interest rates have fallen to 2 percent. Your 4.375 percent yield would look pretty darn good to a buyer. He'd offer you more than $1,000 for you bond.

Bond traders, incidentally, use a more sophisticated measurement, called yield to maturity, to reflect the value of your principal over time. But the principle is the same: Prices rise when rates fall, and vice-versa.

Bonds have long been associated with retirees, because they make fixed income payments, like a pension. (The bond market is sometimes called the fixed income market, for that reason.) As investments, however, they have several interesting properties:

- They are less volatile than stocks, in part because their income offsets price declines. The worst one-year period for the Lehman Brothers U.S. Universal Bond index, for example, has been a 3.49 percent loss in October 1994. Best period: an 18.47 percent gain.
- Bond prices tend to move in the opposite direction from stocks.

This last point bears some explaining. Bond traders are only happy when it rains. To a bond trader, a piece of bad economic news is a wonderful, wonderful thing. Why? Because interest rates fall in a slack economy. Fewer people seek loans when the economy is bad, so the price of money—interest rates—fall. And when rates fall, bond prices rise.

If you follow the bond market, you'll usually see stories that read like this:

Rioting broke out in a bread line Friday, and quickly engulfed all of Manhattan. Bond prices rose.

Conversely, a strong GDP report—or any other encouraging economic news—will send the bond market into a tailspin.

Perverse? Sure. But think of bonds and stocks as opposites. Stocks rally when the economy is strong; bonds falter when the economic numbers are good. And when the economy sputters, stocks fall and bonds rise. For that reason, a portfolio that combines stocks and bonds is typically less volatile than an all-stock portfolio, and higher yielding than an all-bond portfolio.

The typical ratio of stocks to bonds in a conservative portfolio is 60 percent stocks and 40 percent bonds. The longer you have before you reach your goal, the more you should keep in stocks.

Cash: For Money You Need Very, Very Soon

Let's say you're planning to buy a house next year. You've saved $20,000. You'd like to have $25,000. Where can you invest to get $25,000 in a year?

Nowhere, if you can't live with the risk of losing money. When you need a certain amount of money at a certain date in the very near future, you have to accept what savings vehicles give you—and in most cases, that isn't much.

Cash, in Wall Street terms, is any safe investment that can be quickly converted to spending money. In return for safety and liquidity, however, you get smaller returns. How small? At this writing, you can earn:

- 1.92 percent from a money market mutual fund
- 1.89 percent from a three-month T-bill

You can get higher yields by locking up your money for a longer period of time. For example, a six-month T-bill yields 2 percent, and a one-year bank CD yields 3.05 percent, according to Bank Rate Monitor.

You can stretch that rate a bit further by looking for the highest-yielding bank CDs. Bank Rate Monitor's best one-year CD yield is 3.95 percent. But here again, you're taking more risk. Banks that offer the highest yields are generally the ones most desperate for money. Although the Federal Deposit Insurance Corp. insures your deposits to $100,000 (retirement accounts get $250,000 of insurance), it's still no fun to have your bank go under.

Why the differences in bank rates and, say, T-bills? When you buy a T-bill, you're getting a market rate. The government actually auctions off T-bills every Monday, and sets the yields according to the lowest bidder. (It's in the government's interest—and the taxpayer's—to keep debt payments as low as possible).

A bank, however, can offer as much, or as little, as it likes on its accounts. It can offer better rates for bigger investors or lower rates for people in different states. So hunting for higher returns makes sense: You can usually find a bank that's hungry for money. Probably the best place to find high yields is at Bankrate.com—www.bankrate.com.

The real advantage to cash is that you won't lose any money. To return to our example of buying a house, you wouldn't want the stock market to determine what size house you buy. If having $15,000 at closing rather than $25,000 means having no house at all, you're better off sticking with the tiny returns you get from cash.

A Word about Mutual Funds

We've talked here about stock, bonds, and money market instruments as broad asset classes. You can, of course, cobble together a diversified portfolio of stocks or bonds on your own, and many people find that an enjoyable pastime.

On the other hand, most individuals don't, and there's no shame in that. For the vast majority of people, investing in a mutual fund is the easiest way to get a broadly diversified portfolio. For a basic portfolio—we'll talk about other fund strategies in later chapters—you need to know three things:

1. **Avoid highly specialized or faddish funds**. No good ever comes from them. Right now, for example, you can buy a fund called the Market Vectors Global Agriculture fund. (Ticker: MOO. No, really.) It's doing well because food prices are rising. It will do really badly when food prices eventually fall. Just steer clear of these types of funds. You'll have more fun with your money by setting it on fire and dancing around it naked.

2. **Keep expenses low**. Every fund charges fees for its daily operations: Rent, salaries, and advertisements featuring fund managers staring thoughtfully off into the middle distance. These fees are good for the fund industry, which has some of the highest profit margins on earth. But they're not good for you. All things being equal, it's best to keep as much of your money as you can. You can find a fund's expense ratio in its prospectus. You shouldn't pay more than 1 percent for a U.S. stock fund, or 0.75 percent for a bond fund.

3. **Consider an index fund**. These funds ditch the manager and simply track an index, such as the Standard & Poor's

500 stock index. Over time, they will be middle-of-the road performers, but that's better than 50 percent of all mutual funds. And, because index funds have low expenses, they will almost always beat the average stock fund over the long term.

If you're looking for a basic stock fund, consider the Vanguard Total Stock Market Index fund, which tracks the total U.S. stock market. It charges just 0.15 percent a year in expenses, or $15 for every $10,000 invested. Hard to argue with that. Vanguard's Total Bond Index is a good choice for a basic bond fund. It charges 0.19 percent a year, or $19 per $10,000 invested.

Should you buy through a financial advisor? Absolutely, if you feel you need financial advice. You will have to pay for that advice, and typically you will pay through commissions, higher fees, or both—which will eat into your long-term returns. If you're just looking for a basic stock or bond fund, stick with the two funds above, or a similar fund from other no-load companies like Fidelity, T. Rowe Price, or Charles Schwab & Co. You'll save the commission and extra fees, and that's all to the good in the long run.

Your Greatest Source of Wealth

If you remember the days of the great dot-com boom, you probably remember some guy who casually mentioned that he had gotten into America Online or Cisco a few years ago, and has since quit his job. "I'm an investor," he'd say, leaning back against the bar.

Is this a story about schadenfreude? Well, yes. Of course.

AOL, as we know, soared from a split-adjusted price of $2.39 a share to $74.25 a share the end of 1999, a rise of nearly a skizillion percent. The stock—now incorporated into Time Warner—sells for about $16 a share, and the guy you met at the bar is either back at work or living on a diet of boiled gravel and crickets.

If your retirement plan is hitting the next AOL—and, presumably, selling it before it collapses—well, good luck to you. Many people who hit the Big One owe more to luck and random chance than they do to savvy. And, in fact, we often mistake luck for brilliance. Far more companies go under than get big and brawny, and the death rate is cumulative.

Consider this example, set forth in a book called *Fooled by Randomness*, by Nassim Nicholas Taleb, a brilliant market thinker. Imagine a giant Russian roulette game with 10,000 players. Each year, those people would be handed a gun with one bullet in six chambers. If they lived, they would get $1 million. If they lost—well, they lost.

After 20 years, you'd have 313 very wealthy people, and 9,687 very dead people. Would you consider the 313 people smart, and rush to interview them, asking them about their savvy Russian roulette techniques? Probably not.

In reality, you probably won't make that One Big Stock, make a killing, and spend the rest of your life boring people at bars about how smart you are. You'll probably earn an average amount on your investment. That being the case, the biggest single determinant of how much money you'll have in the future is how much money you save. In fact, there's a mildly obscure mathematical rule, called the Millionaire's Estimate, which proves it fairly well. It's an offshoot of the Rule of 72, which is a way to estimate how long it will take to double your money. (Answer: Divide the interest rate by 72. At 7 percent, for example, you'll double your money in 10.3 years.)

The Millionaire's Estimate says that to reach a savings goal you have to save about two thirds of that amount. The rest is covered by interest or earnings. So if you want to have a bit over $1 million, you need to save about $720,000.

Your biggest investment, then, is you. The more money you can earn, the more money you can save. So if you're thinking of taking extra courses, or training for a higher slot on the corporate ladder, you should do so. It will have the highest payoff in the long run.

If you're strapped for cash, or if you simply don't have the discipline to invest regularly, don't bemoan your fate, or your shortcomings. Give the task to someone else. If you have a 401(k) plan at work, sign up for it. Worried that monthly deductions will sap your standard of living? Don't be. You probably won't notice a big difference. If you must, start by contributing just 1 percent of your salary. Then bump it up as often as you can.

This is particularly important if your company matches your contribution. In personal finance, there is an exhaustively researched axiom, called the Free Money Rule. It reads, in its entirety:

Free money is good.

If your company contributes 50 cents for every $1 you contribute, you're automatically earning 50 percent on your money, even if you put it in the most chuckleheaded option in your 401(k). That's better than the performance of—well, just about everyone.

If you don't have a 401(k), don't worry. There are few financial institutions in the world that wouldn't be willing to tap your bank account at regular intervals.

The mutual fund industry, in particular, has many generous automatic investment plans. These not only make it more convenient to invest, but they often drop their minimum investment requirements. T. Rowe Price, for example, the Baltimore-based mutual fund company, normally requires a $2,500 check to open an account. If you open an automatic investment plan, however, you can start with just $50, provided you pledge to keep contributing until you hit $2,500.

How to Put Your Basic Plan Together

You can take two approaches for your basic plan, and both work quite well. The first approach is to assume that you have no crystal ball, and probably won't be able to foretell the market's future any better than anyone else. The odds—and reams of academic research—are with you here.

If you want to invest by the odds, then the odds are reasonably good that, over the long term, stocks will fare better than bonds or cash. The longer the long term—in other words, the more time you have—the better the odds are in your favor.

So if you're a young person out of college, wondering what to do with your first 401(k) savings plan, the answer is simple: Put it in the stock fund option and forget about it. Don't put more than 10 percent into your own company's stock. Remember the AOL guy—or, for that matter, the Bear Stearns guy.

The closer you get to retirement, the more bonds and cash you should have in your portfolio. At 50, for example, you should start adding bonds. If you lose half your money in the stock market at 50, you may never make up that loss. So sometime around the time when you start yelling at kids to get off your lawn and reminiscing about the Good Old Days, you should start moving towards a balanced portfolio—60 percent stocks, with the balance in a mix of bonds and cash.

The second approach is similar to the first. You start by setting broad parameters among stocks, bonds, and cash. For example, at 40 you might decide to be anywhere from 50 to 70 percent in stocks, and 50 to 30 percent in bonds. You tweak these percentages according to their relative value.

Let's go back to the 10-year Treasury note as an example. At current rates, you'll earn 4.06 percent in T-notes, which isn't terribly appealing. If you have a long-term investment outlook, then, you should tilt your portfolio towards stocks. Should T-notes start moving to the 6 to 7 percent range, however, you might consider adding to your bond portfolio.

With either approach, you should rebalance your holdings periodically. If you're aiming for a mix of 60 percent stocks and 40 percent bonds, for example, your mix will soon get out of whack as the market moves. Every so often, you should sell funds that have soared and reinvest into funds that have lagged. You're supposed to sell high and buy low, remember.

If you like, you can pick a day once a year to rebalance— New Year's, or your birthday, or Arbor Day, for that matter. But when you think about it, rebalancing your portfolio according to the Earth's rotation around the sun doesn't make a lot of sense. Instead, rebalance when your portfolio is seriously out of balance. If you're aiming for a mix of 60 percent stocks and 40 percent bonds, for instance, rebalance only when stocks get ten percentage points above or below your target.

The beauty of this approach is that you won't have to rebalance very often—and when you do, it's likely to be when stocks are very cheap or very expensive. A portfolio of stocks and bonds is a remarkably self-balancing mechanism, because the two assets tend to move in opposite directions. If you wait until your portfolio is seriously imbalanced, you will only have to rebalance a few times every decade—and when you do, you will be glad that you did.

That's it. You can, if you like, invest in an asset allocation fund. These mutual funds adjust their mix of stocks and bonds according to your investment temperament—conservative, moderate, or aggressive. A subset of asset allocation funds aim their portfolios at the year in which you plan to use your money—2030, for example—and gradually move from stocks to bonds and cash as the date approaches. These are fine approaches, too.

Chapter 6

What's the Worst That Could Happen?

William Miller, a 19th-century minister, predicted that the world would end sometime between March 31, 1843 and March 31, 1844. His preaching became remarkably popular, and he gathered thousands of followers. When those dates passed, Miller's followers settled on October 22, 1844 as the world's final date, and waited expectantly.

As things turned out, the Millerites were mistaken, and October 22, 1844, became known as "The Great Disappointment." Although a few Millerites remained, trying to refigure their calculations, many others sheepishly rejoined their churches and resumed normal life.

Just why the end of the world is such an enduring fascination is a great mystery. To some extent, people are fascinated by financial collapse for the same reason they enjoy watching movies like *Armageddon*, a mildly dreadful movie about a killer asteroid, or *War of the Worlds,* a pretty good movie about invaders from Mars. People just seem to have a morbid interest in the end of the world, or at least New York City and Tokyo.

One interesting theory: People who are most interested in the apocalypse simply dislike the world the way it is, and would like all the things they don't like to go away. After all, most people who predict the end of the world also offer a way for a select few to avoid the mayhem—and, in fact, to prosper from it. The Pacific cargo cults, for example, believe that foreigners will leave, but that their cargo—manufactured goods—will continue to arrive.

Predicting the end of the world, or at least the collapse of the financial system, seems to be a cottage industry of sorts. It works fine until, eventually, people realize that the world hasn't ended yet and move on, sheepishly, to another advisor. Howard Ruff, a financial guru in the 1970s, rode the wave of collapse in the 1970s with books titled *Famine and Survival in America* and *How to Prosper During the Coming Bad Years.* His newest book is *How to Prosper During the Coming Bad Years in the 21st Century.* "Read why ruinous inflation is on our doorsteps and how to prosper from it," his web site reads.

Of course! Everyone else will be poor, and you'll still be wealthy! The drawback, of course, is that everyone else rarely suffers alone. If you're living the high life in a house on the hill, you'd better have a well-fed army, too.

Even if you could raise an army, it's still a bad idea to base your financial plan on catastrophe. For one thing, true financial catastrophes are relatively rare. For another, very few people actually predict them—and when they do, people usually don't listen.

For example, a few people actually predicted the crash of 1987, when the stock market fell more than 20 percent in one heart-stopping day. James Stack, publisher of the newsletter, *InvesTech Market Analyst,* was one. Another timer, Richard Russell, followed Dow Theory, which looks at how the Dow Jones industrial average relates to the Dow Jones transportation average. Robert Prechter, a student of the often arcane Elliott Wave theory, was the third.

Nevertheless, these were just three of many market gurus operating at the time; many more missed the crash entirely. The odds are much better that you'll pick a market soothsayer who pulls you out of the market in time to miss a big uptrend, and puts you back in just before a bear market.

Putting all your money into one type of investment because you're worried about a market crash is often the single best way to lose money. Everyone worries about a crash. Everyone thinks, at least occasionally, about the end of the world. But that doesn't mean you should position your entire portfolio around an event as difficult to predict as the end of the financial world.

That said, it does make sense to take a few precautions. You might not expect your house to burn down—who does?—but it's generally a good idea to carry fire insurance. Similarly, it's not a bad idea to keep an emergency kit handy: A flashlight, some drinking water, some food, a radio, a spare six-pack of beer. You never know when an earthquake, tornado, or unwanted relatives might find you hiding in a closet for a while.

In our last chapter, we talked about creating a basic portfolio. You'll make more money, by and large, by preparing for good times than by fretting about bad times. Most of your time and attention on financial matters should be spent tending that port-folio. It will probably be the single largest source of your wealth.

But you should take certain precautions against financial catastrophe, and in this chapter, we're going to talk about basic personal finance steps you can take to protect yourself against a reasonably predictable financial problem: Recession.

Downturns in the Upticks

Throughout most of U.S. history, the general direction of the economy has been up. Gross domestic product—the sum of everything produced in the nation—has kept a fairly steady course for the past 70 years or so. (See Figure 6.1.)

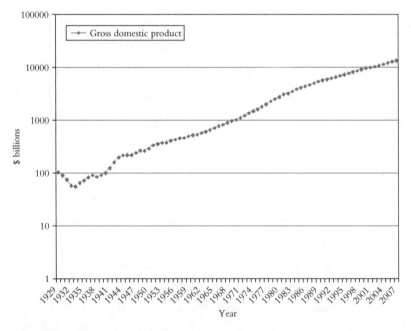

Figure 6.1   Gross Domestic Product
Source: Bureau of Economic Analysis.

Of course, there have been a few noteworthy downturns. For example, November 1973 through March 1975 was a period of significant decline in economic activity across the country. In economics parlance, it was a recession—one of the biggest ones in the past 30 years. Unemployment hit 10 percent, the stock market fell 45 percent, and the nation was engulfed in disco.

A special committee of the Bureau of Economic Research, with the unfortunate name of the Business Cycle Dating Committee, determines when a recession begins and ends. Although you will usually see the definition of a recession short-handed as "two consecutive quarters of negative GDP growth," in fact, the Business Cycle Dating Committee defines it a bit less narrowly. The Committee looks at GDP, real income, employment, industrial production, and wholesale/retail sales.

We call business downturns "recessions" primarily because they don't sound as scary as "depressions," which is what business downturns were called before the Great Depression. After the Great Depression, no one wanted to hear the word "depression" ever again. And with good cause.

In the depths of the Depression, the banking system had collapsed. The Dow Jones industrial average, which hit a high of 382 in 1929, fell to a low of 41 by 1932, an 89 percent decline. Manufacturing and construction slowed to a crawl.

Interestingly, the 19th century had its own version of the Great Depression, a downturn that began in 1836, preceded by wild speculation in real estate, canals, and railroads. The depression of 1836 led to the virtual collapse of the banking system and default by many states on their debt. It was followed by a long period of sluggish economic growth, known as the "hungry

40s," that prompted many families to head West for a new start. So even though depressions of the great variety are rare, don't think that the Great Depression was a singular event. They do happen, from time to time, and you never really know when one will start.

Those Who Fail to Learn from the Past. . .

The specter of economic collapse is always with us: Although the United States took many steps to prevent another Great Depression, no plans are ever perfect. And as the Depression falls from living memory, many argue that the rules put in place to prevent a Depression are antiquated. For example, in the wake of the Depression, Senators Harvey Glass of Virginia and Congressman Henry Steagall of Alabama worked together to create the Glass–Steagall Act, one of the most sweeping financial reform bills in history. Senator Glass's portrait still hangs in the conference room at the Federal Reserve in Washington, watching the proceedings with a wary eye.

The Glass–Steagall Act created the Federal Deposit Insurance Corp., which insures deposits at member banks. We take FDIC insurance for granted, but a run on the bank is no laughing matter: Before the FDIC, your life savings could vanish in an afternoon. Riots would break out when a bank was rumored to be in trouble, and a run was literally that: People ran to get their money out of the bank before it closed its doors. Today, accounts are insured up to $100,000, and retirement accounts are insured up to $250,000.

Glass–Steagall created Regulation Q, the provision that limited the amount of interest that banks could pay, and, most importantly, it prohibited bank holding companies from opening other types of financial services companies—such as investment banks.

Over the years, parts of Glass-Steagall have been picked apart. Regulation Q, as we saw in Chapter 2, fell by the wayside in 1980, thanks to the Depository Institutions Deregulation and Monetary Control Act. And the Gramm-Leach-Bliley Act, passed in 1999, allowed banks to dabble in investment banking.

Gramm-Leach-Bliley may go down in history as deregulation that sounded good at the time, but probably wasn't. The reasoning behind the Glass-Steagall Act was that banks shouldn't be allowed to become too adventurous. When banks stray from banking into other ventures, such as investment banking, they increase the risk that they will fail and, in the process, bring other financial institutions down with them.

Those worries resurfaced during the subprime crisis. In fact, the primary reason that the Federal Reserve intervened in the Bear Stearns meltdown was to prevent the subprime contagion from spreading to the rest of the banking system. After all, many major banks—Citigroup, Bank of America, and JPMorgan Chase among them—had enormous investment banking arms, and all three dabbled in the subprime mortgage business. Already, Treasury secretary Paulson has suggested a sweeping reform of how financial services companies are regulated, with the Fed taking some oversight duties over investment banks.

As the financial system has grown in complexity, however, it has created problems that Mr. Glass and Mr. Steagall couldn't have imagined. Although the subprime crisis may have been contained—thanks to prompt regulatory action—there are always plenty of things to worry about. One of the main worries, lately, has been derivatives.

Broadly defined, a derivative is a legal contract between two parties. The value of the derivative depends on the price movement of something else—for example, a stock, an index, or an interest rate.

A futures contract is a derivative: It's a way to speculate on the future value of commodities, stocks, or interest rates. If you thought the price of corn would rise, for example, you'd buy a contract to deliver a certain amount of corn to a certain place on a future date—which is why they are called futures.

Let's say you decided that corn, currently selling at $8 a bushel, would rise to $9 a bushel in September. You would buy a contract at the Chicago Board of Trade (now the CME Group) to deliver 5,000 bushels of #2 yellow corn in September. Although the contract would be worth $40,000, you'd only have to put down a good-faith deposit of $2,025.

Should corn rise to $9 a bushel, your contract would be worth $45,000, and you could close your position with a $5,000 profit. You would have more than doubled your deposit money. Naturally, should corn fall to $7 a bushel, you would have lost your deposit and more. (Regulations require that your margin remain at least at $1,500, so once the contract has fallen through that level, you would have had to pony up more cash.) Should you forget to close out your contract before the expiration date, you'd be on the hook to buy 5,000 bushels of corn and deliver them—meaning you could lose many times your investments.

Although futures contracts are volatile, they are traded on closely regulated exchanges, and don't seem to threaten much harm except to those who speculate there. And, in fact, futures do perform a useful function—buy shifting risk from farmers and buyers onto speculators. Consider a farmer—outstanding in his field, naturally—who expects to have a corn harvest in September. The price of corn is now $8, and if it rises to $9, he'll be out dancing in his field. If it falls to $7, however, he'll be out of business. He can contract to sell the corn at $8 a bushel now—which is not fabulous, but at least he won't get $7 a bushel.

Many other types of derivatives, however, are not traded on exchanges, and it is these off-exchange derivatives that are worrisome. One reason is that it's hard to know exactly what kind of options are out there. When Bear Stearns was melting down, for example, the market for default swaps in the company's debt swung wildly. These are simply a kind of non-regulated insurance, where one company will pay another if a third company defaults on its debts.

In good times, as insurance companies know, this is an easy way to make money. And, even two years ago, insuring against a Bear Stearns default probably seemed like a lay up. Who could imagine that Bear Stearns, the fifth-largest investment bank in the nation, would default on its debt? As the company's problems surfaced, however, the annual cost of insuring $10 million of Bear Stearns debt soared from less than $100,000 to more than $700,000. Had Bear actually defaulted on its debt, it's doubtful that all the insurers would have been able to actually pay off.

Other derivatives are even more exotic, and are limited only to the imagination of those who create them. Inverse floaters, for example, are notes whose interest rates rise when a benchmark yield falls, and vice-versa. You can buy derivatives whose value depends on inflation, or pollution, or even the weather.

All of these might seem like harmless fun among companies with more money than sense, except for two things. The first is the staggering size of the derivatives market: One estimate of the notional value of derivatives is more than $500 trillion. (One should be skeptical of any estimate of value larger than $60 trillion, which is roughly the world's gross domestic product. Nevertheless, the derivatives market is astonishingly huge.)

The second is called counterparty risk, which is why Warren Buffett, CEO of Berkshire Hathaway and the nation's wealthiest man, called derivatives "financial weapons of mass destruction." Put simply, counterparty risk is the risk that the other person involved in a derivatives deal won't be able to pay as promised. Suppose, for example, that you had owned $10 million of Bear Stearns debt and had decided to buy a credit default swap from SomeYahoo, Inc., just to be on the safe side. So you paid SomeYahoo $100,000—about 1 percent—to insure your bonds.

Had Bear Stearns actually defaulted—and it didn't—you would have depended on SomeYahoo to come up with $10 million. If SomeYahoo couldn't do that, it would go out of business. And, quite possibly, so would you. The great fear in the derivatives market is that something, somewhere, could spark a huge chain reaction of defaults, sending companies into sudden and unexpected death spirals.

And, frankly, the debt market alone is worrisome enough without adding derivatives to the mix. What made the Bear

Stearns meltdown so frightening was its potential to spread to the bond and money markets. Bear Stearns didn't collapse because its stock price fell: The company's stock price simply reflected Wall Street's view of the company's worth, which, in turn, was based on its value at a forced liquidation auction. In a bankruptcy, stockholders are at the end of the line. The company's bondholders determine who gets paid, and there's almost never anything left for stockholders.

Bear Stearns fell because no one would lend the company money when it needed it the most. The risk of losing the entire loan was simply too large. For nearly all companies, the access to credit is the difference between life and death. One default can lead to another, as creditors frantically try to get their money back. When companies start defaulting on debt, and lenders stop lending, the economy grinds to a halt. Broadly speaking, it was a meltdown in the debt market that worried the Federal Reserve, not any problems in the stock market.

Even more specifically, the Fed was also worried about a meltdown in the short-term debt market, called the money market. This is the market for short-term loans between banks and companies. Defaults in the money market can be catastrophic, because they leave companies—and their counterparties—without the money they need for daily operating expenses.

The money market evolved because companies often have large inflows of cash that they don't need to use immediately. Rather than leave $10 million gathering dust in a no-interest bank account, a company could invest it overnight and earn interest at, say, a 2 percent annual rate. If you earn 2 percent on $10 million in the course of a year, your company has an extra

$200,000—enough to buy your CEO that car of his dreams. Or, pay a bonus to a few key employees.

Similarly, a company may have a big bill—let's say $10 million to keep it simple—coming due on Tuesday, but not enough cash to pay the bill until Friday. It can borrow the $10 million at a fairly nominal rate and pay its bills on time, thanks to the money market.

Money market investments come in all different flavors. Commercial paper, for example, is a kind of short-term IOU issued by highly creditworthy companies. Repurchase agreements, discussed in Chapter 4, are short-term contracts to buy and sell securities. Banks will offer short-term certificates of deposit, called jumbo CDs that offer modestly higher interest rates than what they offer the hoi polloi. And the U.S. Treasury is always glad to borrow money via its weekly auctions of Treasury bills.

Although many companies and banks invest in the money market, the odds are good that you do, too. Money market mutual funds, which currently have more than $3 trillion in assets, buy money market securities and distribute the interest to investors. Unlike all other kinds of mutual funds, money funds keep their share price at $1 every day, and pay interest in fractions of shares. By keeping the share price at $1, investors don't lose money.

But there's no guarantee that a money fund will keep its share price at $1. The industry has a remarkable history of safety: Only one small institutional money fund has ever had its share price fall below $1. The few times when a major money fund has gotten stuck with a default, the fund's sponsor has waded in and added enough cash to keep the share price at $1. No one wants a run on the money market, least of all the

Federal Reserve—which is another reason the Fed was so concerned about Bear Stearns.

Bear, like most investment banks, was an active player in the debt market and the money market. Furthermore, it was a big player in the market for asset-backed commercial paper, much of which was backed by mortgage-backed securities. Fortunately for everyone involved, the asset-backed commercial paper withstood the subprime market admirably. The banks that guaranteed the asset-backed paper paid off when they had to, and money funds were smart enough to stick with only the top-rated asset-backed commercial paper. No money fund was harmed in the subprime meltdown.

Worries about the debt market, and the money market, are the kinds of things that keep Federal Reserve chairmen up at night. Stock meltdowns make the Fed uneasy, but debt liquidation is the stuff of Fed nightmares. It was, ultimately, a destruction of the credit markets that created the Great Depression, and if there is to be another Depression, it will be because of the credit markets too.

Your Mother (or Grandmother) Was Right

If you knew someone who lived through the Depression, you know that it was an experience that left a deep mark on them. Sure, they may joke about having boiled gravel for Sunday dinner or having to share a pair of shoes among 17 children, but times were indeed hard. Consider this: The school lunch program, a fact of life for kids since the 1940s, evolved because so many potential recruits for World War II were turned away because of malnutrition.

One hallmark of the Depression generation was a great fear of debt. There are two reasons for this. First of all, the Depression was deflationary: That is, prices fell continually throughout the worst of the depression. This might seem swell to you, particularly if you've filled up your gas tank recently. But when prices are falling, debt becomes increasingly onerous. Suppose your debt payments are $100 a month. As prices fall, the value of that $100 rises each month: You're repaying the bank with increasingly valuable cash.

The second reason is a bit more obvious: If you lose your job, your debts will overwhelm you quickly, as many borrowers have discovered during the subprime crisis. Missed payments means, eventually, bankruptcy and foreclosure and misery. Even worse, filing for bankruptcy today is much more onerous than it was just a decade ago. You may not be able to file Chapter 7 bankruptcy, which eliminates most debts. And under the bankruptcy laws passed in 2005, you'll have to pay more to file for bankruptcy.

The first step to ensure your financial safety is to pay down your debts. Thanks to the near-disappearance of usury laws, you can pay 30 percent or more on credit cards. If you make the mistake of going to payday lenders (motto: "Really, we're not as bad as loan sharks!"), you could wind up paying 400 percent or more.

All things being equal, repaying a credit card that charges 30 percent is the equivalent of earning 30 percent on your investments. But repaying a debt has even greater rewards, as we shall see.

Let's say, for example, that you owe $10,000 on your credit card, and that your interest rate is 21 percent. Your minimum payment each month is 4 percent of your balance—after interest, of course. In one month, you're paying $175 in interest alone. Your monthly payment is $407. We'll also say that if 4 percent of your balance is less than $25, you have to pay $25. At that rate, it will take you 12 years to pay off your debt. In the meantime, you will have paid your credit card company $7,275 in interest, which is why you get all those flyers in your statements saying how much they enjoy the relationship (See Figure 6.2.) Really, they should be sending you flowers.

As we noted earlier, paying off the debt is the mathematical equivalent of earning 21 percent—this is, if you had suddenly come into a windfall of $10,000, your return from using it to pay off the debt would be the same as earning 21 percent. In reality, however, your return is much higher.

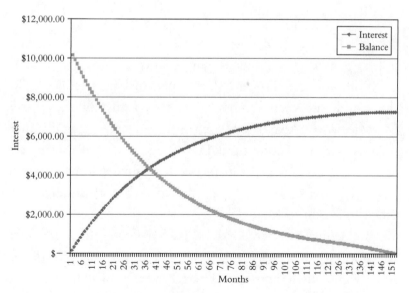

Figure 6.2 Interest on $10,000 Credit Card Charging 21% Annually

Most people operate under a cash flow model, rather than a balance-sheet model. In other words, when you eliminate a $407 debt, you have $407 extra dollars in your pocket that you can use on other things, such as gasoline, food, shelter, or investments. And by paying off that debt, you have that $407 extra dollars pretty much forever—unless, of course, you decide to get into debt again.

And this is where you start to have to make some hard choices. After all, unless you were utterly feckless, you got into debt because your spending exceeded your income. In the words of Mr. Micawber, from Charles Dickens' novel, *David Copperfield:*

> "Annual income twenty pounds, annual expenditure nineteen nineteen six, result happiness. Annual income twenty pounds, annual expenditure twenty pounds ought and six, result misery."

In other words, if your expenses exceed your income by just six pennies, the ultimate result is misery.

Now, you can line up all the personal finance books in the world, and their essential advice isn't any different from Mr. Micawber's: Live below your means. As with many maxims, such as "Keep a happy thought," "Work hard and play hard," and "Don't stick your head in the fish tank," Mr. Micawber's advice is easier said than done. (Mr. Micawber, we should note, didn't follow his own advice.)

Budgeting, to a large extent, is like dieting. It's not much fun until you can get some results. Your first step: Work up some righteous indignation. The easy target, of course, is that any company would willingly charge 20 to 30 percent or more on a credit card. These companies will say, of course, that they have to charge higher interest rates to make up for defaults, as well as for those people who pay their bills promptly and don't incur any interest charges.

Oh, boo hoo. As far as defaults go, part of the job of lending money is evaluating the creditworthiness of those to whom you lend. If you're doing such a poor job of credit research on your customers that you're stuck with deadbeats, well, you've discovered an important lesson about the nature of your business. Lending involves risk, and it's the lender's job to control that risk. Don't blame your customers for your own mistakes.

And, sure, some people are diligent and pay their bills on time. Generally speaking, that's considered a virtue. More importantly, most credit-card companies compensate for their customers' virtue by the fees they charge to merchants. Ask a gas station owner sometime how much he pays per gallon for credit-card fees.

So start by getting mad. Why should you help any company that's gouging you for 21 percent interest? Isn't that just wrong? Aren't they just taking money from you? Shouldn't you form a big crowd and storm their headquarters, dragging their leaders off to the Bastille and . . .

Ok, not that mad. But you should be angry enough that you resolve to pay these guys as little as possible. You can start by picking up the phone, calling your credit-card company, and asking for a lower rate. Many times, the conversation will go like this:

You: Could I have a lower interest rate?
Credit-card company: No.
You: Ok, thanks.

Nevertheless, if you've been a good customer—and you mention that you might want to go to another bank's lower-interest card—then the credit card company might indeed give you a lower interest rate. It's worth asking.

If you do decide to find a lower-rate card—always a good idea—make sure you're not replacing a high-interest card with a high-fee card. One of the best places to shop for a new card is at www.bankrate.com. If you do get a new card, remember that those zero-interest offers have a limited lifespan—at which point they soar to the normal rate.

More importantly, you should become very aware of your credit card's policies on late payments, which you'll usually find on your statement in type that's roughly this size. Once you've found it, you'll find that the company will hit you for an additional $30 or so for a late payment. It might increase your interest rate, or take away your rewards points. It could also ding your credit report, which means you will pay extra for other loans. All because you paid late.

So make sure you pay on time. One easy way is to set up an automatic billing feature, where you can send your credit-card payment to the company precisely on time. Most banks now offer this feature for free; many credit-card companies do, too.

Ideally, however, you should use a credit card for convenience and pay your bill in full and on time. Easier said than done? Sure. But let's address the problem in two ways.

Step 1: Paying Off the Card

The problem with paying the minimum on a credit card is that your grandchildren will be grown by the time you pay off a big balance. And shoveling all your money to the credit-card company will leave you bitter. Also hungry. Here's one suggestion: Pay this month's minimum until the bill is paid off. In our example, you'd repay your debt in a bit less than three years.

If that seems too onerous, try paying this month's minimum for the next 12 months. After 12 months, you can pay the minimum payment again: $282. You've given yourself a $125 pay raise.

Twelve months later, your payment will be $196—$86 more than the previous year, and $211 more than when you started. After five years, your debt will be down to $1,600 and your payments will be about $65, which should be comfortable enough for you to manage until you finally pay it off.

The gradual approach has three big benefits:

1. It pays down your debt more quickly than paying the minimum each month.
2. It rewards you every year for your efforts. This is important: The advantage to getting out of debt is having more money to spend on things you want.
3. It enables you to save a bit of money every month.

Step 2: Building up Some Savings

The reason you have credit card debt is because you're living beyond your means—or at least, your expenses have overwhelmed your income. This probably isn't because you're driving a Mercedes, smoking $100 stogies, and buying a new pair of shoes every three days. One of the difficulties of making a budget is the sudden, unexpected expense.

If you're a homeowner, for example, you may suspect that there is a sensor hidden in your furnace that detects when your savings account balance rises above $400. At that point, a very vital part—the transcendental nebulator, perhaps, or the infindibulum valve—goes out of balance, creating a negative vacuum in the air pump and causing the entire heating system to go out of balance. You then call the HVAC guy, who charges you $700. The HVAC guy won't take your word that you will pay him Tuesday, so you reach for the plastic.

Cars, too, have a similar sensor. Get more than $200 in your bank account, and your transmission will become stuck in hyperdrive, and the mechanic will have to re-install the Sonic Gofaster gear at a cost of $1,000. Once again, the plastic will have to come out.

The solution, of course, is to try and have enough savings to cover the inevitable appliance or automotive breakdown. If you use the gradual method for paying down debt, you can sock away your savings and build up a rainy-day fund. In your second year, for example, you'd have $1,500—enough to fix an infindibulum with some left over for a new microwave.

Otherwise, you have to resort to old-fashioned thrift. It's surprising how quickly you can accumulate savings, because it's remarkable how many companies work so hard to take your money from you.

Once again, attitude is important to succeed at saving money. It's not going to work if it just makes you bitter. And there are so many other things to be bitter about—why waste all your hard-earned bitterness on something that can't feel your bile? For example, if you keep the thermostat down to 62 in the winter, you'll be a bit richer, but you'll also be cold—and lonely, since your friends won't visit you, unless they happen to be penguins.

If, however, you feel that every step you take will not only make you happier, but stick it to all those companies trying to take your money—well, all the better. One easy step: Buy a new automatic thermostat. You can program it to fall to 60 when you're away, and move back up to room temperature 15 minutes before you return. You can even get some thermostats that you can control from your work computer, which could also lead to some interesting practical jokes on your teenagers.

Buying some items in bulk, such as pet food, tuna fish, paper goods—really, anything non-perishable—is also a good idea. You will save money running to the store when you run out of food for Fido, and you will save money on your grocery bill. The savings from places like Costco and Sam's Club really does add up. If your cat eats a can of food a day and you pay 75 cents, you're paying $273.75 a year. Buy it at a discount club for 50 cents, and you're saving $91.25 a year. You should be able to save $500 to $1,000 a year by buying in bulk.

Similarly, look carefully at some service bundles that your telephone or cable company might offer. Although they are never the $99 they advertise—they always neglect to mention the fees for connecting the services, renting cable boxes, and reversing the flux capacitor on your mandingo—you will usually get a good price for long distance, telephone, and television services.

Clearly, you don't want to get to the point where you're molding soap slivers into Christmas presents or re-stuffing your sofa with cat hair. That's just wrong. But if you figure that saving just $5 a day will net you $1,825 a year—well, there's nothing wrong with that, especially if it means you can pay cash for the things you really want.

How much savings is enough? Asking that question of a financial expert is a bit like asking a dentist how often you should floss. The normal answer is that you should have about six months' of expenses stashed somewhere where you could tap it in an emergency. That's not the same as your salary: After all, you won't have to pay taxes on your savings when you withdraw them.

The amount varies, of course, by your profession. If you're a nurse, for example, you can probably find a job more easily than if you're a journalist or a buggy-whip maker. Can you ever have too much money stashed away? Why, no, you can't.

Which Card First?

Let's say your $10,000 in credit-card debt is spread among three cards, each with different interest rates and balances. Which one should you pay off first?

Experts are split on this one. One strategy says that you should pay off your smallest balance first, because it will give you a feeling of achievement. This may be true, but your biggest savings will be from attacking your biggest bill. For example, let's say your biggest credit card bill is $7,500. You also have a $2,500 card. The payment on the large bill is $305; on the smaller one it's $102.

If you keep paying $305 a month for 12 months on your larger bill, you'll have an extra $93 a month after the first year. You'll only save $32 a month by using the same technique on the smaller bill. It makes more sense to pay aggressively on the larger bill, rather than the smaller one.

In a desperate situation, you could try taking out a home equity loan and paying off the credit cards. This assumes three things:

1. You have a home.
2. You have equity in your home—typically, at least 10 percent of the home's value.
3. You have a lender willing to make a home equity loan. Thanks to the subprime meltdown, they're not as anxious to make home equity loans as they used to be.

The advantage is that you'll get a lower interest rate, and the interest you pay will be tax-deductible. Should you sell your house at a profit, you'll be able to eliminate the debt entirely.

The disadvantages? If you pay the loan over 10 years, you're still going to pay a lot of interest, tax-deductible or not. And if your borrowing problems are structural and you don't address them, you've put your house at risk. Should you get into credit-card trouble again, you'll have no other recourse—and if you fall behind on your home equity loan, you could lose your house to foreclosure.

No Debt Ever?

One of the latest personal finance fads is the no-debt movement. This means paying off your credit cards, your car loans, and your mortgage, too. Is it a good idea?

In the best of circumstances, auto loans are good things to avoid. You shouldn't borrow for an asset that doesn't appreciate, and your average car is worth less every year. At the end of the loan payment, your bank has your money, and you have a klunker.

Unfortunately, it's not easy to get the $10,000 or so you'll need for a car that doesn't start with a crank. Your best move is to buy as little car as possible at first, take as small a loan as you can, and save for your next one.

Generally speaking there's no great virtue to owing the bank for 30 years for your house. Even though the interest is tax-deductible, a person in the 25 percent tax bracket is only saving 25 cents in taxes for every $1 he spends on the mortgage.

If you can afford the higher payment, a 15-year mortgage is a good thing, particularly if you plan to retire in the reasonably near future. A paid-up house is a true joy when you're retired and on a fixed income.

But if you have a 6 percent mortgage and you're considering paying it down aggressively—well, forget it. If paying down a 21 percent credit card is the equivalent of earning 21 percent, then paying down a 6 percent mortgage is the equivalent of earning 6 percent. And in most cases, you can do better than 6 percent elsewhere.

The main advantage to paying down debt, of course, is to have more to invest. But low debt is also a good safety strategy. Should the economy go into an extended downturn, your best defense is to keep your debts at a minimum and your savings at a maximum.

Chapter 7

Fighting Depression

If you ever go to Yellowstone National Park, you'll be awed by its majestic peaks. You'll gasp at the jets of steam that burst out of the ground. You might even feel a mild earthquake or two, which are quite common in the area.

The park was a hit with geologists almost since its discovery. Whatever in the world could cause such an interesting combination of high-temperature geysers and earth tremblors?

What, indeed. Recent studies of Yellowstone have shown that the park sits directly atop a volcano. And not your run-of-the-mill, bury-a-few-villages type of volcano, either. No, Yellowstone is a gargantuan supervolcano, whose caldera, or crater, is more than 1,500 square miles in area. The caldera of Mount St. Helens, which blew its stack memorably in 1980, had an area of just two square miles.

Intrigued, geologists investigated the area around Yellowstone further, and discovered that the last time the supervolcano erupted,

640,000 years ago, it flung 8,000 times more ash into the atmosphere than Mt. St. Helens did, covering vast swaths of the West. How often does this happen? About every 600,000 years. We're about 40,000 years overdue.

Fortunately, in geologic time, 40,000 years is a blink of an eye, and volcanoes don't work on anyone's clock but their own. At the moment, geologists see no signs that another Big One is coming down the pike.

The financial system, too, is sitting atop its own supervolcano: An enormous mountain of debt. Most people rail about the federal debt, and that is, indeed, enormous: $9.4 trillion, according to the Bureau of Public Debt.

A trillion dollars is, of course, a huge number. To give you some idea: A billion seconds ago, the nation was celebrating its bicentennial. A trillion seconds ago, people were still hunting mastodons with flints.

Of course, all things are relative. A million dollars of debt isn't too bad if you have $10 million in the bank. It's horrendous if you have $100,000 in the bank. But even relative to the nation's gross domestic product—our total output of goods and services—the federal debt is enormous. The government expects that its total debt will be 69 percent of gross domestic product in 2009, the highest amount ever.[1]

To finance the debt, by definition, we have to borrow. In the first quarter of 2008, the U.S. Treasury borrowed $149.4 billion, or $10.8 billion a week, by issuing Treasury securities. U.S. investors don't buy all those Treasuries. The debt is so enormous that we have to rely on foreigners to buy our debt—which they have done so far. Japan, for example, is the largest foreign holder of Treasury securities, to the tune of $592 billion. Mainland China has $502 billion. Oil exporters have $153.9 billion.[2]

A truly cheesy movie, called *Rollover*, focused on what would happen if, suddenly, foreigners no longer wanted to buy all our debt. (*Rollover* focused on what would happen to the banking system if foreigners yanked their deposits, but it was the same idea basically.) In order to get people to buy our debt, the government would have to offer higher interest rates on Treasury securities. And that, in turn, would mean higher rates for just about everything, from car loans to mortgages. Already, interest rates in the U.S. are about a percentage point higher than they would be if we were a debt-free society.

States, towns, and other municipalities are also big debtors, albeit not as big as the federal government is. State debt is about $2.2 trillion.

But there's much more debt out there than what the government owes. Walk down any suburban street, and you'd be hard-pressed to find any large object that's not bought on credit. In 2007, Standard & Poor's chief economist David Wyss calculated that household debt was 137 percent of after-tax income. Debt payments are now about 19 percent of the average household's after-tax income, Wyss said.[3]

If you add up all the debt in the U.S. credit market, it comes to about $45 trillion, according to Ned Davis Research. That's about three times U.S. gross domestic product. To give you some idea of how incredibly unbalanced our books are, total debt was about 1.6 times GDP in 1929, on the threshold of the Great Depression. The ratio ballooned to 2.6 times GDP at the height of the Depression, as the government spent and borrowed madly to prop up the economy.

Drowning in Debt

The sheer, staggering size of the debt in the U.S., both public and private, raises disturbing questions. What would happen if the U.S. was hit by a depression? The government might not have enough borrowing ability to lift the nation out again. What if there was another war the size of World War II? Where would the government get the money to finance it? And how would ordinary individuals fare in a debt meltdown? If the subprime crisis is any indicator, we have an answer: Not well.

Let's scare ourselves for a moment and consider some of the worst possible outcomes from our national debt binge. We'll start with the scariest one, which is debt liquidation.

In its shortest form, debt liquidation is simply an out-of-control chain of defaults. How could that happen? Let's say that a very large investment bank fails. We'll call it Stare Burns & Co. In this example, the government feels that it has no business keeping a company from failing. After all, if the government bails out every business that makes a mistake, businesses would feel that there's no penalty for mistakes, and they would continue to make mistakes until the government is bankrupt.

So Stare Burns joins the vast business boneyard. It sells off all its assets, including its big building in Manhattan, and tells creditors that it can only pay 40 cents on the dollar. Stockholders get nothing.

Right after the announcement, the Dow Jones industrial average falls 2,000 points. Banks stocks are particularly hard hit. Investors rush to sell their stocks before losing more money. Suddenly, every stockowner is 10 percent poorer.

Those companies that own Stare Burns bonds, however, are 60 percent poorer. Many companies can take that kind of hit. But a few can't. They had counted on Stare Burns paying its debts, and now they need a new source of funding. Like a ship that jettisons cargo when it's taking on water, these marginally solvent companies have to start selling assets so they can pay their debts.

Alas, a few companies fail—typically, not because they owned Stare Burns bonds, but because they counted on Stare Burns' business. They, too, default on their debt, and their stock becomes worthless. In a matter of days, other companies begin folding, as more and more debt becomes worthless. Lenders, worried about making loans in an economic downturn, stop accepting loan applications.

In the meantime, shell-shocked stockholders are realizing that, while their assets have fallen, their liabilities remain the same. Some well-heeled bankers who could afford a big house in the Hamptons before the Stare Burns meltdown find that they can no longer do so now. They, too, begin defaulting on their debts and frantically try to liquidate assets. But right now, everyone is a seller, and no one is a buyer.

As companies begin to shut down, consumers instinctively curtail their spending. Retailers cut prices, but to no avail. In fact, as prices fall, consumers spend less, assuming that the price will be lower later. As the economy falls into a deepening gloom of bankruptcies, people begin hoarding what little money they have, figuring that there will be worse times to come.

Some economists would argue that this scenario, as frightening as it is, is actually good for the economy. At the very bottom, all the crummy debts have been liquidated, and the economy can rise once again from the ashes, shaken but strengthened and operating on a more sound financial footing. These are the same people who feel that caring for the homeless means stepping over them, rather than on them.

In theory, the institutions we have from the last Great Depression are in place, and stand ready to act. When Bear Stearns looked like it was about to topple, regulators stepped in to make sure that the contagion didn't spread. (We should note here by the way, that this was a very bipartisan action: Treasury Secretary Henry Paulson, no fan of government intervention, played a key role the sale of Bear Stearns to JPMorgan Chase.)

The collapse of the Depression hit so hard because so many institutions proved so fragile. Banks failed, leaving depositors penniless; brokerages did, too, with the same effect. (Brokerages are now covered by SIPC insurance, which will replace securities in a failed brokerage account.) Nevertheless, it's conceivable that a future Fed might not be as inclined to step in—or than some exogenous event, starting somewhere else in the world, could start a debt liquidation that would spin out of control.

A Lender Be

We talked about the importance of reducing your debts in the last chapter. In general, the less debt you have in a debt liquidation, the better off you are. In deflation, your income will fall, but your debt payments will remain the same. To keep up with payments, you'd have to cut back in other areas—going out to eat, buying new clothes, or traveling, for example. Eventually, the interest payments would become too much, and you'd have to default.

Being on the other side of the equation as a lender, however, would be the best situation. You'd get a stream of payments, and, because prices were falling, you could buy more with your payments each month.

But there's a big drawback with being a lender in a deflationary spiral, which is that your borrowers are increasingly likely to default. In that case, you'd lose your entire investment, even if you resorted to methods that would earn you nicknames like "Mr. Potter," or "Knuckles." Would there be some way you could get a steady stream of payments without worrying that the payer will shuffle off to oblivion?

One easy answer is a Treasury bond, which is a long-term loan to Uncle Sam. You could get higher interest rates if you invested in corporate bonds, but if you're trying to hedge the effects of a deflationary recession, then you want Treasuries. Why? Because corporations can go bankrupt. The Treasury, on the other hand, is the safest credit risk in the world. If the Treasury goes bankrupt, well, you have more problems than the value of your bond—like whether it's better to hole up in the hills, or raise your own army for self-defense. In times of true economic worries, the whole world flocks to Treasuries.

First, let's have a brief word on nomenclature. Strictly speaking, a Treasury security that matures in one to 10 years is a Treasury note; one that matures in more than 10 years is a Treasury bond. If it matures in one year or less, it's a Treasury bill.

You buy a T-bill for less than its face value, which is called buying it at a discount. When the bill matures, you get its full value; the difference is your interest. The discount rate actually understates your interest rate. If you buy a $10,000 one-year T-bill at a 4 percent discount, you give the Treasury $9,600.

A year later, you get $10,000 back. Your interest is $400 on $9,600, which is actually a 4.2 percent yield.

Treasury notes and bonds make semi-annual interest payments. Let's say you invested $10,000 in a 10-year T-note, which matures on May 15, 2018. Its coupon is 3.875 percent, which means that the government will pay you $387.50 every year until it matures, at which point you'll get your money back.

Treasury securities have one additional charm: Interest is free from state income taxes. The federal government and the states have a deal: The Feds don't tax income from state bonds, and the states don't tax income from federal bonds. If you live in a state with high income taxes, such as New York, California or Maryland, then you get an added benefit from owning Treasuries. If you live in a state with no income taxes, well, you just get a warm tingly feeling from owning the safest securities on the planet.

In a depression, bond prices would soar. Each successive payment on your bond would be able to buy more goods and services, and investors would be clamoring to buy your bond. For example, suppose you bought a 10-year Treasury security that had a coupon yield of 4 percent, or $400 per $10,000 bond. Two years later, yields dropped to 3 percent. Your bond would be worth $10,768—a 7.68 percent gain. (We're being fancy and using yield to maturity here because, well, we can.) The more yields dropped, the more valuable your bond would become: (See Table 7.1.)

The longer the maturity of the bond, the greater the price gains. Table 7.2 shows the same example, using a 30-year T-bond instead of a 10-year T-note. Once again, two years have passed since the bond was issued.

Table 7.1   Price of a $10,000 T-Note with Coupon of 4% when Yields Fall

Yield	3%	2%	1%
Price	$10,768	$11,663	$12,721
% gain	7.68%	16.63%	27.21%

Table 7.2   Price of a $10,000 T-Bond with Coupon of 4% when Yields Fall

Yield	3%	2%	1%
Price	$ 11,156	$13,302	$16,386
% gain	11.56%	33.02%	63.86%

You would only realize these gains if you sell your bond, and if you sell your bond, you'll have to reinvest it at a lower rate. Nevertheless, if you wanted to use your bond as security for a loan, you could use the higher price to value it. You would be wealthier, which is unusual in a depression, to say the least.

The risk: If rates rose, your bond would be less attractive to other investors, and you'd have to cut your price to sell it. To use the example in Table 7.2 above, let's say you invested $10,000 in a 30-year T-bond with a 4 percent coupon. Two years later, rates rose to 6 percent. Your bond would be worth $7,409.

But remember: You're buying this primarily as a sort of insurance policy against deflation. If the nation doesn't endure a soul-searing economic downturn, you'll still earn 4 percent on your money, and get your principal back when your bond matures.

But still, you say, $10,000 is a lot to tie up for 30 years, and 4 percent sure isn't much. Is there any cheaper way to get inflation protection? Sure: Zero-coupon bonds.

A zero-coupon bond, as its name implies, doesn't pay annual interest. Instead, the bonds are sold at a deep discount to their value at maturity. Old-style savings bonds were sold the same way: You'd pay $25 for your bond, and the government would give you $50 when the savings bond matured.

Just how much you pay for a zero depends on the term, as well as the interest rate. For example, a 30-year zero-coupon bond with a face value of $10,000 and a 4 percent interest rate would cost you $3,083. A 10-year zero-coupon bond paying 4 percent would cost you $6,756.

Long-term zeros are probably the cheapest and most effective way to hedge against deflation. Let's say you bought the 30-year zero in the illustration above, and that its yield was 4 percent. If rates were to fall to 2 percent, your bond would jump in value to $5,521—a 79 percent gain.

Just as with regular bonds, there is an equal and opposite reaction should interest rates rise. Bear in mind, however, that as long as you hold your bond to maturity, you won't lose any money.

Zeros have one other problem: You're taxed on the interest as if you received it every year—which, of course, you don't. So you should keep your zeros in a tax-deferred account, such as an individual retirement account. Even better, put them in a Roth IRA—you won't owe anything on your earnings if you have had the Roth for five years and you're at least 59 ½ when you take your withdrawals.

Treasury securities of all stripes do have one small tax advantage: The interest they pay is free from state taxes. This is part of a longstanding deal between the states and the federal government. The Feds don't tax interest paid on state bonds, and states don't tax the interest on Federal debt securities. If you live in Texas, which has no state taxes, the state tax benefits of Treasuries won't interest you one bit. If you live in New York or California, however, the exclusion of Treasury interest from state taxes is a nice thing indeed.

The best way to buy Treasury securities is through the Treasury Direct program. The feds will wire interest and principal payments right to your bank account, and there are no fees. You can find out more about Treasury Direct at www.treasurydirect.com. If you want to buy zero-coupon bonds, however, you'll have to go through your bank or broker.

Even if you're using Treasuries as a form of insurance against deflation, don't get carried away—particularly when rates are extremely low. Five percent of your portfolio is enough if you use zero-coupon bonds. If you're particularly worried, you might put another 5 percent of your portfolio in short- to medium-term Treasuries and have it do double duty as your rainy day fund. After all, Treasuries are extremely liquid, even in the worst of times, and can be a good source of emergency money.

When rates are very low—as they are at this writing—you probably don't want to buy Treasuries with maturities greater than five to seven years. One good strategy is to ladder your maturities, which is simply a fancy way of saying that you should buy Treasury securities of varying maturities. For example, rather than putting $10,000 into a 10-year T-note, consider putting $4,000 in one-year T-bills, buying one $1,000 T-bill every three months. Buy $3,000 in three-year notes, $2,000 in five-year notes, and $1,000 in a 10-year note. If rates rise, you'll be reinvesting your one-year T-bills at increasingly higher rates. If rates fall, at least you'll have some money earning higher yields.

Leading the Charge: Utilities

A deflationary depression is one of the nastiest of all economic environments. In a truly bad outbreak of deflation, Treasury securities or insured bank accounts are about as risky as you want to get. In fact, during periods of high financial anxiety, people sometimes accept T-bill yields that are less than the rate of inflation just because they want to make sure they get their money back.

On the other hand, fairly long periods of mild deflation are somewhat more common than full-blown depressions, and while they're not a lot of fun, they're not the end of the world either. Japan, for example, has slogged though a multi-decade deflationary period. Although its stock market has gone nowhere, and rates are low, the country has done fairly well, all things considered.

In a deflationary period, economic activity is slow, and the Fed will typically lower interest rates to try and get it going again. That's good for Treasury bonds, as we noted above. It's also good for stocks of utility companies.

Utilities pay above-average dividends, which is one reason retirees love them. For example, the 25 largest U.S. electric utilities pay an average 3.7 percent, according to Standard & Poor's. The average company in the S&P 500 pays about 2 percent. Because utilities aren't growth companies, they pay out a larger percentage of their earnings to shareholders than, say, Google or Yahoo!, two big Internet companies. And as interest rates fall, the yields on utilities look increasingly attractive to investors.

Furthermore, while utilities suffer in a downturn about as much as any company, people still need power, telephone service, and water, even in a recession. Unlike companies that produce high-heeled clogs, utilities always have big demand.

One nice feature about utilities is that, with time, you can get a large yield on the amount you initially invest, provided you reinvest the interest for a while. For example, suppose you had invested $5,000 in Southern Co., a middling performer, 10 years ago. Assuming you reinvested your dividends, your stock would be worth $10,870 now. The stock has a 4.8 percent dividend yield, so you would get $521.76 a year in dividends, which is swell enough. On your $5,000 initial investment, however, you're getting a 9.58 percent yield. It's hard to beat that.

If you don't have the inclination or the patience to invest in individual utility stocks, you might consider a utility fund. You'll get a slice of a diversified portfolio of utility stocks for a fairly low price.

Utility funds have two drawbacks. One is that funds typically take their annual expenses from the dividends on the stocks in their portfolio, so most utility funds don't have particularly good yields. American Century Utilities, for example, has a yield of about 2 percent, or about as much as a money market fund.

The other drawback, peculiarly, is that there really aren't many good no-load utility funds. A load is a sales charge, or commission, and when you buy a fund through a broker, you can pay as much as 5.75 percent in commissions. You buy no-load funds directly through the fund company, bypassing both the load and the broker. Normally, there's little difference in performance between no-load and load funds. After all, the funds don't differ in how they are managed—they differ in how they are sold.

That said, every no-load utilities fund tracked by Morningstar has a below-average five-year record. American Century Utilities is the top-performing no-load utilities fund, and it ranks in the 53rd percentile of all utilities funds—which is to say, it's just slightly below average. It has averaged a 17.63 percent return the past five years, including reinvested dividends.

The top-performing fund is MFS Utilities, which has gained an average 24.38 percent the past five years and yields 1.93 percent. Even if you paid the full 5.75 percent sales charge, however, you would have fared better with MFS than with American Century.

Bargains for the Brave—and the Liquid

In a deflationary environment, prices for everything fall. Nowhere is this more true than for stocks. When the worst is over, you can often find huge bargains.

In 1939, Sir John Templeton, founder of Templeton funds, borrowed money to buy stocks that sold for less than $1. Nearly all of them made money. His best stock, Missouri Pacific Preferred, sold for $1/8. He sold it for $5, a 3,900 percent gain.

Of course, we're talking about John Templeton here, one of the greatest investment minds of the past 100 years. But great catastrophes can make for great bargains. In August 2002, during the nuclear winter for technology stocks, we looked at technology stocks you could buy for less than $5 a share. A few, such as Sanmina, just got worse. The circuit-board maker fell from $3.54 a share to $1.50. Others, however, did quite well. Software maker CompuPower, for example, soared from $3.63

to $10.19; Corning, which makes fiber optic cable, rocketed from $1.98 to $27.30.

There's much more to finding bargains than buying the stocks on the list of companies making new lows. Many stocks that fall below $5 have a ticket on the Doomsday local to $1 and from there it's just a short hop to the corner of First and Eternity. Nevertheless, if you have cash on hand, and you're both brave and patient, you can sometimes pick up great bargains when everyone else is despondent.

Real estate, too, is an area where you might be able to find bargains. As foreclosures increase, banks and desperate owners are often glad to sell at highly reduced prices. The drawback: you'll probably have to pay cash, because in a true economic downturn, you'll have a tough time finding a lender. And, because the real estate cycle tends to be much slower than the stock market cycle, you'll have to expect to hold on to your property for a long time before you can sell and make a profit.

You might also consider real estate investment trusts, or REITs, but only after the downturn has been under way for a long time and shows signs of recovery. REITs invest in commercial property, and by law, they have to pay out nearly all their after-tax profits to shareholders in the form of dividends. As a result, REITs, like utilities, typically have above-average dividend yields, which make them attractive in deflationary times.

Unfortunately, deflation means lower prices, particularly for real estate. So if you move into REITs during a deflationary period, you're entering the realm of speculation: You're betting that the worst is over. There's nothing wrong with optimism, but make sure you're being optimistic, not credulous. Even when prices have fallen 50 percent, there's nothing to say that they can't fall another 50 percent. One of the wonders of math and finance is that prices can fall by half virtually forever.

Exotica

Thanks to the wonders of Wall Street engineering, you have plenty of ways to make money—in theory—from worldwide global depression. Whether you could make money in reality is another question.

In recent years, exchange-traded funds have become an enormous hit, in large part because of their many advantages. ETFs are, first of all, index funds: That is, they don't have a fund manager, but simply try to track a stock or bond index. (In England, they're called, logically enough, tracking funds.) Like most index funds, ETFs typically have very low annual expenses—an enormous advantage over most actively managed funds. The less you give to your fund company, the more you get to keep.

The largest ETF, the SPDR trust, tracks the S&P 500 stock index. But you can find ETFs that track virtually every index on the planet, from the widely diversified Wilshire 3000 to the insanely specialized Claymore Global Timber index.

What makes an ETF different is that it's traded on a stock exchange, rather than purchased from a mutual fund company. If you were to buy the Vanguard 500 Index fund, a garden-variety mutual fund, you'd have to contact Vanguard and buy shares through the Valley Forge, Pa. company. When you buy or sell, you're limited to the fund's closing price that day: You can't bail out during the trading day.

But ETFs are traded throughout the day—in theory, you could trade ETFs all day if you had the time and the inclination.

You can also sell ETFs short, which is a way to make money on falling prices. When you sell an ETF short—or a stock, for that matter—you borrow shares from your broker and sell them. If the stock falls, you can buy shares at a lower price, return the shares to your broker, and pocket the difference.

For example, suppose you thought the stock market was going to fall. You borrowed 100 shares of the SPDR Trust at $140 a share, and sold them on the market, for a cost of $14,000. Just as you surmised, the stock market fell, and SPDR Trust shares swooned to $120 a share. You wade back into the market and buy 100 shares at $120, repay your broker, and keep the difference of $20 a share, or $2,000. Should the stock market rise instead of fall, you'll take a loss, and sometimes a big loss. After all, the most you can lose on a stock is 100 percent, but in theory, a stock can rise forever.

ETFs do have one big advantage for short-sellers, however: They are exempt from the uptick rule. Many years ago, short-sellers would pile on to a distressed stock, pushing its price down mercilessly. To prevent that, exchanges now require that you can only short a stock when its previous trade was an uptick. You can't just short a stock as it plunges. But you can, however, short an ETF as it falls, which gives ETF short-sellers a bit of an advantage.

Each time you trade an ETF, you have to pay a broker's commission, which makes them impractical for people who like to invest a bit at a time. But if you have a lump sum that you want to invest for the long-term an ETF is a good way to go.

Because the stock market has been so choppy of late, many fund companies have trotted out bear-market ETFs. The Short S&P 500 Proshares fund, for example, rises when the stock market falls, and vice-versa. The Ultrashort S&P 500 Proshares fund is designed to rise 2 percent when the S&P 500 falls 1 percent, and vice-versa. One can only imagine that the Ultra-ultrashort S&P 500 fund is just around the corner.

If you were extremely worried about depression and deflation, your thoughts might turn to a bear fund or an ultrabear fund. A small investment in a bear fund, for example, might offset the losses in your stock portfolio. You run into three problems here, however.

- **Timing**. To use a bear fund most effectively, you have to be willing to try and time the market. If so, you're trying to do what a vast amount of research has shown to be impossible. If you do attempt to time the market with bear-market ETFs, you should be willing to monitor your investment closely, and to bail out when it looks like the market is moving against you. Good luck with that.

- **Pain**. Let's say that you decide to keep a small amount of your portfolio in a bear-market fund as a sort of insurance policy. To make this an effective strategy, you have to be willing to pour more money into your bear fund when it loses money. And, in most cases, it will lose money: The stock market rises much more than it falls. The average bull market since 1900 has lasted about 1,300 days, according to the *Stock Trader's Almanac*. The average bear market, by contrast, has lasted 406 days.

- **Liquidity**. Exchange-traded funds use a mechanism to make sure that their share prices stay closely in line with the index they track. The mechanism works best when volume and liquidity is high. At times when the market is moving very quickly, thinly traded funds can vary substantially from their index—meaning that the gains you expect might not be the gains you actually get.

You may, however, be able to profit from long-term deflationary trends by investing in EFTs that bet against commodities. Unfortunately, there aren't any, primarily because the market for commodities has been so hot.

A few companies offer exchange-traded notes that bet against commodity indexes, but ETNs might not provide the comfort you need in a severe deflationary environment. An ETN is backed only by the word of the company that issues it. Should the issuing company disappear, well, so would your investment. Typically, companies that issue ETNs are highly regarded Wall Street firms. Why, one ETN is named the BearLinx Alerian MLP Exchange-Traded Note. Yes, that Bear— Bear Stearns. Although the note is still traded, presumably through JPMorgan Chase, the ETN itself should serve as a bit of a warning, particularly if you're planning on using it as a defense against a major deflationary cycle.

Who's Afraid of the Big, Bad Bear?

Of all the things to worry about on this planet—floods, war, another season of American Idol—a major deflationary depression is admittedly low on the list. The Federal Reserve can, theoretically, do anything short of throwing money out of helicopters to avoid a monetary collapse. (Ben Bernanke, the current Fed chairman, has earned the nickname "Helicopter Ben," by referring to the use of a "helicopter drop" of money to get the economy going. In fairness to Bernanke, he was referring to a Milton Friedman quote.)

Nevertheless, it's conceivable that a major deflationary spiral could begin elsewhere and spin out of control so fast that monetary authorities aren't able to keep up with it. Even that, however, is fairly unlikely. Central bankers around the world tend to be a single-minded bunch, and allowing a debt liquidation to spread would be anathema.

What's more likely is a long period of mild deflation caused by a global slowdown in growth. In Japan, the big deflation in real estate prices led to vast amounts of problem loans. Banks then had to increase their reserves for loan losses, which, in turn, reduced the money they had available to lend. And by importing cheap goods from China, Japanese producers had to continually lower their prices to remain competitive.

Sound familiar? But Japan has had several factors that have prolonged their misery. For one thing, Japanese banks have been slow to write off problem loans, instead keeping them on their books for decades. In the U.S., banks tend to be more ready to cut their losses and move on. Furthermore, because the Japanese banking system is so troubled, many Japanese don't trust the banks with their savings. Instead, they buy U.S. Treasury bills or gold, which means, again, that their banks don't have as much money to lend.

Whether deflation is fast or slow, the best protection for your portfolio is probably Treasury bonds. If deflation does occur, you'll get gains in the price of your bonds, and you'll get regular interest payments as well. If all goes well, you'll still get regular interest payments, and there's nothing wrong with that.

If you talk to your grandparents, however, you'll also find that the best protection against a major economic downturn is not your portfolio, but your friends and family. During the Depression, people didn't hole up in their houses, horde food, and take potshots at strangers. To the extent that they could, people helped each other through hard times. And in truly hard times, that's really the best you can hope for.

Chapter 8

Creeping Inflation

O ne of the enduring moments in *The Rocky and Bullwin-kle Show* was the episode involving the Pottsylvania Creeper—a rapidly growing plant that invaded the sleepy town of Frostbite Falls, Minnesota.

Although the Pottsylvania Creeper bore more resemblance to Audrey II, the carnivorous plant in *Little Shop of Horrors*, it also bore a strong similarity to the kudzu vine, which was planted throughout the South in the 1930s through the1950s. Kudzu, an import from Japan, was promoted as a vigorously growing plant that would help stop soil erosion. Kids working in the Civilian Conservation Corps planted it; park rangers planted it; people even formed kudzu planting societies.

Unfortunately, kudzu grew to love the South more than the South loved kudzu. In particular, kudzu loved the South's warm, humid climate, its temperate winters, and its appealing lack of natural enemies. Soon, kudzu was embracing entire forests, overrunning houses and burying cars and tractors, too.

In recent years, the South has come to love Kudzu, which may have medicinal properties and makes swell cattle feed, too. But people still tell their children to keep the windows shut at night, so the kudzu doesn't creep up on them.

Inflation, too, is a creeping menace, and one that some people might even embrace, at least at first. But of all the dangers investors face in the wake of the Bear Stearns collapse, inflation is probably the largest.

The Spiral

Inflation is the gradual erosion of the buying power of money. Over the past decade, inflation has averaged 2.9 percent— reasonably low, by most standards. But when you think of inflation on a 12-month basis, you overlook its real ravages. Inflation's effects are cumulative after all. Devalue your currency a bit every year, and the end result is an enormous devaluation over time. For example, suppose you retired a decade ago, and your living expenses were $1,000 a month. To buy the same items—food, fuel, clothing—you would need $1,329 today, according to the Bureau of Labor Statistics.

Naturally, when inflation is higher, its effects are even more profound. The consumer price index, the government's main gauge of prices, has risen at a 4.7 percent annual rate the past 40 years. If your living expenses were $1,000 a month in 1968, you'd need $6,225 today to buy the same goods and services.

The 40-year average rate is higher than the 10-year average because of the extraordinary inflation spike in the 1970s. Consumer prices gained an average 7.9 percent a year in the 1970s, and soared 13.5 percent in 1980. Inflation was the economic event of the 1970s, and it left a lasting impression on anyone who lived through it. People still fretted about it even in the 1990s, when inflation was comfortably below 4 percent for the entire decade. (See Figure 8.1.)

Economists still debate over what caused the inflation in the 1970s, Most likely, it was combination of governmental mistakes and huge, outside forces.

The primary cause of inflation in almost any period is lax monetary policy by the central bank, lax fiscal policy by the government, or a combination of both. Monetary policy deals with the control of the money supply and interest rates, and is the province of the Federal Reserve Board. Fiscal policy is controlled by Congress, which can raise or lower tax rates.

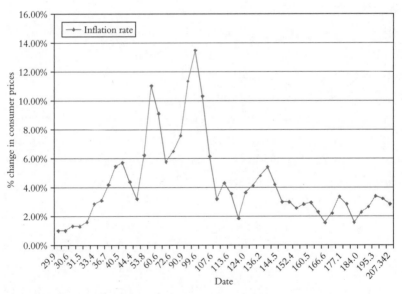

Figure 8.1 Inflation Rate: Year-Over-Year Change in the Consumer Price Index, 1961–2007
SOURCE: Economic Report of the President, 2008, table B80.

153

The great economist Milton Friedman said, "Inflation is always and everywhere a monetary phenomenon."

Put simply, inflation begins when the government creates too much money. If you increase the amount of money in while the amount of goods and services remain the same—or don't rise as fast as the increase in the money supply—then prices typically rise. The Fed did just that in the early 1970s.

The federal government can stimulate the economy by increasing spending, lowering taxes, or both. Raising taxes or cutting spending tends to slow the economy. When the government overspends for a long period of time, it can also increase inflation, simply by overstimulating the economy. Fed economists have argued that, as long as the Fed is independent and well run, it can override fiscal policy and keep inflation under control.[1] This is a bit of a tautology, and even most die-hard central bankers will admit that their job is much tougher if they have to fight over controlling inflation with Congress.

Some also argue that war is inflationary, primarily because it requires so much government spending. War also takes people from the workplace, restricts the free movement of goods and services, and drives up the demand for certain goods, such as steel, lead, and khaki. Inflation has followed most U.S. wars, particularly the Revolutionary War and the Civil War, but also World War I and Vietnam, as well.

In any event, by pumping money into the system, the government puts the economy into overdrive. Interest rates fall, companies borrow and expand, and consumers borrow more to buy more stuff. Eventually, demand for goods and services outstrips the country's ability to produce them, forcing prices up.

As prices rise, workers start demanding higher raises. And, because the economy is booming and labor is scarce, companies give out those higher raises. They pass on the added cost to consumers in the form of higher prices, and the cycle begins all over. The result is a classic wage/price spiral: Wages and prices feed on each other, each driving the other higher.

When Prices Rise, Prices Rise

The inflation of the 1970s was made worse by an exogenous factor: soaring oil prices. The Arab oil embargo began in October 1973 as a byproduct of the Yom Kippur war and the United States' support of Israel. In response, Arab oil producers raised prices 17 percent and cut production. In November 1973, Mideast oil producers cut output by another 25 percent.

Aside from causing long lines at the gas station, higher oil prices sent consumer prices soaring across the board. Oil is a commodity that's involved in the manufacture of many things, from fertilizer to plastics to fabrics, and as oil prices rose, so did the price of many other goods as well.

Economists debate whether or not the 1970s inflation was caused by higher oil prices—called a "cost-push" inflation—or whether inflation was purely a monetary phenomenon, sometimes called "demand-pull." (Some, like Friedman, would argue that there's no such thing as cost-push inflation. High growth spurs demand, which pushes up oil prices. Friedman, apparently, didn't have to fill his tank in the 1970s.) In any event, the 1970s were the harshest period of inflation in the U.S. in the 20th century.

Other countries, however, have had far harsher inflationary outbreaks, which is what really strikes terror into the hearts of central bankers. The most celebrated inflation episode was in Germany between the two World Wars. During the Weimar Republic in 1923, priced doubled every two days, and Germany issued a 1 trillion Mark note. People would use older currency to light their stoves, because the paper was cheaper than firewood. Just recently, Zimbabwe's inflation topped 24,000 percent, according to its government, and many there suspect that the government is downplaying the real inflation rate, and that it's really running at 150,000 percent.[2]

The cure for inflation is almost as painful as inflation itself. Basically, you have to slow the economy enough that demand falls and unemployment rises, squashing upward price pressure. Many times, this means recession. In the late 1970s and early 1980s, the Federal Reserve pushed up interest rates to slow the economy and wring inflation from the system. By 1981, the prime rate—the rate at which banks lend to their most credit-worthy customers—soared to 18.9 percent. The discount rate rose to more than 13 percent. A three-month T-bill yielded 14 percent.

In the course of wringing out inflation, the Fed caused a severe recession. The unemployment rate climbed to 9.7 percent in 1982, the highest since the Great Depression. The stock market plunged in 1981, and gold prices soared. Not until late 1982 did the economy settle back into recovery.

The Case for a Comeback

At this writing, inflation has gained 4.2 percent the past 12 months, which is well above the Federal Reserve's comfort level, but nothing like 1970s-style inflation.

Nevertheless, you can make a powerful case that inflation could once again raise its ugly head. Start with the massive federal debt, which we discussed in the last chapter: $9.4 trillion, equal to 69 percent of the nation's gross national product. Even though the federal deficit—the annual amount we overspend our national income each year—is shrinking, the deficit continues to grow, in part because of the interest that we owe on it.

The country can deal with the deficit in one of three ways:

1. Control spending and hope that eventually, the debt will become a smaller percentage of GDP. This solution won't eliminate the debt, but it will make the debt more manageable.
2. Slash spending, increase taxes, create a government surplus, and pay down the debt aggressively. People like to propose slashing government spending that doesn't affect them, and raising taxes on other people. Normally, however, a politician who proposes higher taxes or lower spending finds himself looking for a job after the election. In recent years, neither approach has had much success in getting past Congress.
3. Gradually increase inflation, allowing the country to repay its debts with steadily cheaper dollars.

Almost invariably, when confronted with similar choices about repaying national debt, countries have opted for the third solution: Inflation. In its crudest form, governments would simply mix in a bit of copper with gold coins, making more money available. But the debased currency would be worth less. Interestingly, when this happens, people hoard the older, purer currency and spend the new, cheaper stuff. One of the oldest economic maxims, Gresham's law, states that "Bad money drives out the good." It was first formulated in the 16th century.

And why not inflate your way out of a deficit? After all, inflation is often politically popular, at least at first. It doesn't require spending cuts or higher taxes. The average working person would get higher wages to offset higher prices. And his mortgage payments would remain the same, giving him more disposable income.

Farmers, too, would enjoy inflation, for much the same reason. Inflation would boost the cost of crops and farmland. Companies could raise prices. The people who get hurt the most are the poor, who, by definition, don't get big raises, and those who live on fixed pensions. For this reason, inflation is often called "the cruelest tax."

The Fed, of course, stands firmly against inflation, and is determined not to let the inflationary forces of the 1970s return. When asked why inflation shouldn't be allowed, Fed officials whip off their glasses, get right in your face, and start yelling, "You want a piece of this, punk? Do you?"

Ok, they don't do that. But the Fed's mandate is to keep prices stable, and they take it quite seriously. In fact, by the time you read this book, it's likely that the Fed will have started nudging the fed funds rate higher in an effort to ward off inflation.

But there's a wild card involved now, just as there was in the 1970s: oil prices. At this writing, the price of a barrel of oil is more than $130, the highest ever, even if you adjust for inflation. Although the nation is more fuel-efficient than it was in the 1970s, oil is still involved the production of nearly everything.

A Congressional mandate to increase the use of ethanol, made from corn, has helped push up prices even more. As more corn goes to fuel, supplies shrink and prices rise. Food riots have become commonplace around the world. In Mexico, for example, people have rioted over soaring tortilla prices. And corn, as the celebrated book, *The Omnivore's Dilemma,* points out, is in everything from clothes to food to fuel. And, as corn prices rise, farmers plant more of it—and less of other grains, like wheat, pushing wheat prices up. Bakers are getting it coming and going.

Economists argue that high oil prices, by themselves, reduce demand and result, ultimately, in lower oil prices. And this is quite true: At $4 a gallon, people drive less, drive more slowly, and feel the urge to park the Hummer in a high-crime area with the keys in the ignition. Nevertheless, the process of demand destruction, as it's called, is a slow one: You can't just decide not to drive into work any more. It takes a while to replace the nation's fleet of SUVs with more fuel-efficient hybrids. The backyard oil fountain, however, is probably a thing of the past.

The other wild card is this: It's a global economy, and the Fed can't control many things outside U.S. borders. Some other central banks, such as those in Europe, are also committed to controlling inflation. Others, however, are more committed to economic growth, and among these we may include India and China, two of the most voracious consumers of raw materials on earth. Now, this is a good thing: People in what used to be called less developed countries are prospering, and that means that they are eating better, getting better medical care, fooling around with more sophisticated electronic devices, and driving more, too.

Those higher living standards come with a price, which is greater demand for natural resources: Oil, steel, concrete, copper, lead. Demand from India and China has pushed up copper prices to the point where people are stripping old houses for copper tubing. A 2008 U.S. penny, which is now 97.5 percent zinc and 2.5 percent copper, is still worth less than a penny—about half a cent. But a dollar's worth of pre-1983 pennies, which are about 63 percent copper, is worth $2.57.

Does the Fed like this? No. Can the Fed control China's economic growth? Not really. Furthermore, as hedge-fund manager John Rogers points out, you can't just snap your fingers and open up a new copper mine, or a new lead mine. Even assuming you know where a vast amount of copper is, it can take years to get clearance from local authorities to open a new mine. There's a considerable lag between a burst of new demand and the ability to fill that demand, at least when it comes to basic materials.

So even if you can't make the case for hyperinflation—and, thank goodness that seems like a very remote chance indeed—you can make the case that inflation rates are likely to be higher in the next 10 years than they were in the past 10 years. And you can also make the case that a short-term spike in inflation is quite likely. The question, then, is what you do about it.

A Three-Pronged Approach

By and large, a long-term investment mix of stocks and bonds, which we talked about in Chapter 5, is a good way to beat inflation over time. In most cases, you will still make money after inflation with stocks.

Nevertheless, inflation devastates bonds, even during a period of mildly rising inflation. When inflation rises, remember, the Fed raises interest rates to slow the economy and squash rising prices. And rising rates are to bonds as daylight is to Dracula. If you own a $10,000, 30-year bond that yields 4 percent and rates rise to 6 percent, your bond is worth $7,858—a 21 percent decline.

From the early 1950s through the 1970s, bonds were called "certificates of confiscation" because interest rates gradually rose and their real return—adjusted for inflation—was negative.

Big bursts of inflation are bad for stocks, too, in large part because when inflation rises, the Fed raises interest rates. Higher rates mean a slower economy and lower corporate earnings. In addition, when rates rise risk-free savings vehicles, like bank CDs and Treasury bills, look more appealing in contrast to stocks.

What's an investor to do? The traditional investment for rising inflation is gold. But inflation has risen steadily since gold's peak in 1981, and gold certainly hasn't kept up. Gold is an important element in your inflation-fighting portfolio, but you should probably have two others. One is inflation-adjusted Treasury bonds, which are guaranteed to beat inflation. The other is international bond funds, whose exposure to foreign currency will offset declines in the value of the dollar—another side effect of inflation.

Gold

People have prized gold for centuries as a currency. It doesn't rust, it's easily portable, and, with a bit of effort, it's not that hard to tell if someone has tampered with it.

In modern times, gold has become the currency of last resort. It's what you buy when you think that your own government's money will become worthless. In wartime, for example, people horde and bury gold, particularly if they think their side is losing. If your government disappears, after all, your currency and your savings will, too.

When inflation soars, gold often does, too. After all, inflation makes your dollars worth less. As paper assets become increasingly less valuable, people switch to hard assets, such as gold and silver, because they retain their value.

Bear in mind that gold is for preserving your purchasing power, not necessarily for getting rich. If gold far outpaces the rate of inflation, it's probably in one of its periodic bubbles—and it would behoove you to go out and sell all the gold you own. Supposedly, an ounce of gold has been enough to buy a good men's suit since Colonial times. At current prices, that's about correct. When gold was at $250 an ounce a few years ago, you may have had to have shopped a bit harder.

So how do you buy gold? You have several options.

Gold Futures. When you hear the price of gold quoted in the news, it's typically the price of gold in the futures market. A futures contract, as you may recall, is the obligation to deliver a certain amount of gold to a certain location at a set date. Because you can buy a contract for just a fraction of the price of gold, you can make enormous bets on gold prices with very little money.

Most investors, however, would have more fun with their money by renting a convertible, driving down a main street in a crowded city, and throwing it out the window. Small amateur investors tend to lose early and often in the futures market. And remember, your aim is to preserve the buying power of your cash, not corner the gold market.

Gold Mutual Funds. Most gold funds invest in the stocks of gold mining companies, not the metal itself. (There are exceptions, which we'll get to in a moment.) By and large, this can be an excellent way to make money in gold, but it also has some drawbacks.

On the one hand, gold mining stocks can soar when the price of gold rises. That's because it really is a good thing to own a gold mine. Suppose you own the Big Whoopie Gold mine. It costs you about $400 an ounce to dig the gold out of the ground, purify it, and get it to market. When gold is at $425 an ounce, your gross profit per ounce is $25 an ounce, or 6.3 percent.

Now let's say the price of gold rises to $500 an ounce. Suddenly, your earnings have soared to $75 an ounce, or 200 percent—an increase that's far larger than the rise in the price of gold. As you can imagine, such a jump in earnings will translate into a much higher stock price.

Because you can hold a gold fund in your brokerage account, or simply in your own name through a no-load fund family like Vanguard or Fidelity, gold funds are a convenient way to invest in gold. So what are the drawbacks?

- **Wall Street**. Gold mining stocks, like any other stock, don't really reflect the price of gold. They reflect where Wall Street thinks the price of gold will be in six to eighteen months, and Wall Street, as we all know, isn't always an accurate barometer of future prices. So even if the price of gold rises, your gold funds might not rise or fall as much as the price of gold.

- **Inflation**. Bear in mind that true inflation destroys the value of all paper money. When inflation is particularly severe, people won't trust a stock certificate any more than they trust a $100 bill. If you're truly worried that hyperinflation will strike, then a gold fund will do you little good.
- **Gold coins.** A more practical way to own gold is gold bullion coins, such as U.S. Eagles or Canadian Maple Leafs. The advantage: Coins don't need to be assayed for gold content and purity, and they're easily portable. (A London good delivery bar, the kind you see in movies, weighs 400 troy ounces, or 27.4 pounds. Try hiding that in your pocket.)

U.S. gold Eagles are a popular choice; they're 22-karat gold and easy to buy. (The American Buffalo one-ounce coin is 24 carats.) If you can't afford a one-ounce gold coin, you can buy Eagles in weights of a tenth of an ounce, a quarter ounce and half an ounce.

You'll pay a bit extra for the government's seal of approval. Eagles typically sell for 3 to 6 percent more than the spot price of gold. Silver fans can also buy U.S. silver Eagles or bags of pre-1965 silver coins. A bag of $1,000 in face-value silver coins weighs 55 pounds, so be sure to stretch before hauling them home.

What about rare coins? Although a silver standing liberty quarter is a thing of beauty—Augustus St. Gaudens designed them—they are also expensive. You will shell out a large premium for a coin in good condition, and coins that are in anything less than perfect condition are worth far less than top-grade ones. You really need a very special set of skills to create a valuable coin collection—and rare coins won't really address the investment problem you're trying to solve. In times of high inflation, you won't want to sell your coins for paper money. And if you overpay for your coins, you'll never recoup your costs.

Take physical delivery of your gold. You really don't want someone else to hold it for you. Store your coins in a bank safe-deposit box, because gold coins are as portable for thieves are they are for you. If you don't trust banks, you'll have to work out a way to protect your coins from theft, preferably some way that doesn't involve guard dogs, guns, and digging holes in the dead of night.

Another good way to invest is through gold exchange-traded funds. These funds buy gold bullion; one share is worth one-tenth of an ounce of gold. StreetTracks Gold Shares (ticker: GLD) and iShares Comex Gold Trust (IAU) are the two largest gold ETFs.

Take some TIPS

Treasury Inflation-Protected Securities, or TIPS, are long-term IOUs issued by the government, just as other Treasury securities are. You collect interest until they mature, at which point you get your money back. The government guarantees interest and principal.

The twist with TIPS: The government adds principal value monthly to your bond, depending on the percentage change in the CPI. Even better, the government uses the CPI calculation that includes food an energy, rather than the core CPI, which economists prefer. (Core CPI strips out food and energy, because those segments are so volatile. Although economists argue that core CPI is a more accurate barometer of inflation, what it really measures is how infrequently economists go to the grocery store.)

Your interest payments are based on the new, higher principal. The interest rate you earn is set at auction, as with any Treasury security. If you buy your TIPS directly through the Treasury at auction and hold them until maturity, your investment will beat the CPI over the term of the TIPS. For details on how to buy TIPS at auction, go to www.savingsbonds.gov.

Please note that despite the Web address, TIPS aren't the same as inflation-adjusted savings bonds. I-bonds also increase in value according to changes in the CPI, but their current base interest rate isn't very appealing. It's zero. You get the CPI and nothing else. You're much better off investing in TIPS.

You can also buy TIPS through your broker. When you buy through your broker, you get the current market price of the bond. The problem: Many TIPS buyers are convinced that inflation is on the rise, too. In 2007, in a particularly perverse market reaction to inflation fears, TIPS prices were so high that they actually yielded less than the rate of inflation.

Currently, the 10-year TIPS yield is about 1.05 percentage points to 2.19 percent above inflation. That's not bad, particularly if you're worried about safety. To find what Wall Street thinks the real inflation rate is, subtract TIPS yields from Treasury yields. (See Table 8.1.) One caveat: Your additions to principal are considered taxable income in the year you receive it.

You can also buy mutual funds that invest in TIPS. As with all funds, but particularly with bond funds, you should take a

Table 8.1 TIPS Yields

Maturity	TIPS yield	Treasury yield	Implied inflation rate
5 years	1.05%	3.59%	2.54%
10 years	1.70%	4.17%	2.47%
30 years	2.19%	4.73%	2.54%

SOURCE: Bloomberg.

hard look at inflation. If your yield is 2 percent, you don't want to give 1 percent—half—to your fund company. One of the best, low-cost TIPS funds is the Vanguard Inflation Protected Securities fund. It charges just $20 for every $10,000 invested.

Foreign Currencies

Even though gold is considered the world's default currency, it has a rival: the U.S. dollar. Because the U.S. has emerged as the world's only superpower, people trust the dollar nearly as much as gold. A few countries, such as Panama and Ecuador, use the dollar interchangeably with their own currency. Many others, such as Hong Kong, Saudi Arabia, and China, link the value of their currency to the dollar. In times of true world distress, such as the outbreak of war, people tend to buy dollars, not gold.

And, in fact, the dollar and gold tend to move almost precisely in opposite directions. When the dollar rises, gold falls, and vice-versa.

But a fall in the dollar is another form of inflation. When the dollar tumbles, it becomes far more expensive to go abroad. When a Euro is worth 90 cents, a 5-Euro latte at Starbucks in Paris will set you back $4.50. At $1.50 per Euro, the same cup of java will jolt you for $7.50.

More importantly, a weak dollar means that goods imported to the U.S. are more expensive. While we export our debt to other countries, we import inflation from elsewhere.

Fortunately, you can profit from the decline in the dollar if you buy investments that are denominated in foreign currencies. Suppose you had bought 100 shares of the fictional Brussels Grouts, a plumbing supply firm, for 15 euros a share. At the time, 1 Euro equaled $1.10. So your purchase cost was $1,650. Now, the stock is still selling for 15 euros a share, but a Euro is worth $1.47. Your investment is now worth $2,205, even though the stock's share price hasn't budged.

So one way to hedge the effects of inflation—and the falling dollar, is to increase your international investments. For example, you should have about 10 to 20 percent of your stock portfolio devoted to international stock funds. Two suggestions: Fidelity International Discovery (ticker: FIGRX), which has been in the top 25 percent of all international blend funds the past five years, and Vanguard Total International Stock Index, which features rock-bottom fees and sharp performance (ticker: VGTSX).

Other ways to benefit from a falling dollar:

- A dollar bear fund. PowerShares DB U.S. Dollar Index Bearish fund (ticker: UDN) is designed to fall when the U.S. dollar rises in value, and vice versa. It uses futures and other sophisticated strategies to move inversely to the buck.
- A bank CD denominated in foreign currency. EverBank (www.everbank.com) offers CDs denominated in more than a dozen currencies. If the dollar falls against those

currencies, you'll earn interest—and get a boost from the currency effect, too.

- An international income fund. These funds invest in foreign government bonds and are less volatile than international stock funds. American Century International Bond (BEGBX) is a good place to start; so is T. Rowe Price International Bond (RPIBX).

Even though the Fed stands ready to fight inflation, it has considerable headwinds against it. Without help from fiscal policy with Congress, the Fed will have to contend with spiraling deficits and a falling dollar. And without coordination from other central banks—particularly in India and China—the Fed might not be able to fight soaring commodity prices, either. And the soaring price of oil might be beyond the Fed's capacity to fight at any rate.

Will there be soaring, 70s-style inflation, or crunching, 30s-style deflation in the future? We certainly hope not. But today's global economy seems increasingly like a car going 90 miles an hour in a rainstorm at night. Bad conditions don't guarantee an accident, but they make it far more likely.

You should never listen to pundits who tell you to take all your money and invest it to protect against, or profit from, any one scenario. Odds are good that after a few years, they will simply admit, sheepishly, that they were wrong and that they are very, very sorry about all those losses you took in precious metals, ostrich farms, or Caribbean cattle farms.

Your best strategy is to assume that everything will be all right in the end. There's no need to throw out everything you know about investing. Start with a core mix of stocks, bonds, and money market funds that's tailored to your investment goals.

Then add investments to protect yourself from at least some of the dangers we could face in the next couple of years. Spread your investments as widely as possible: Gold, international funds, and TIPS. If all goes well, your insurance investments won't soar in value. But used judiciously, they won't drag down your overall returns if all goes well. And that, perhaps, is the best-case scenario.

Appendix

Take a Load off Fannie

We've talked a bit about Fannie Mae and Freddie Mac as cornerstones of the mortgage market. Now, alas, we have to talk a bit about Fannie Mae and Freddie Mac as symbols of the great Mortgage Meltdown, once-great companies that, like Bear Stearns, became the objects of governmental intervention.

One place to start is with their names. Companies don't usually have cute, anthropomorphic names. Sure, you will have hair salons named Curl Up 'N' Dye, diners called the Dew Drop Inn, and piano movers called Deathwish Piano Movers. But you usually don't get companies that go from the First Bank of Blue Plains to Bobbie Blue.

Fannie Mae gets its name from its ticker symbol, FNM, which stands for the Federal National Mortgage Corp. But the stock was such a solid, blue-chip performer that New York Stock Exchange floor traders gave it the affectionate nickname of Fannie Mae. Similarly, Freddie Mac's symbol, FRE, was the root for its name.

Floor traders aren't a sentimental lot, and most of the nick-names they give to stocks are not fit for a family personal finance book. Microsoft's nickname, for example, is Mister Softee, and we will presume it's named after the ice cream and leave it at that.

But Freddie and Fannie's nicknames stuck, so much so that eventually, they changed their stodgier (yet far more informa-tive) real names to their nicknames. The question then arises: What did Fannie and Freddie do that made them so endearing?

In a word, they produced a string of spectacular earnings that, in turn, translated into soaring stock prices. On the face of things, spectacular earnings from either company is some-what unusual. As you might recall from earlier chapters, Freddie and Fannie purchase mortgages from banks and package them into mortgage-backed securities, for which they charge a fee. They guarantee timely interest and principal on the loans—for which they also charge a fee.

This is not a business with huge profit margins. Fannie's profit margin in 2002 was 7.5 percent; its highest profit mar-gin was 15.7 percent. Those are not bad margins—certainly not grocery-store levels—but certainly nothing like Microsoft, which reliably has margins in the 20 to 30 percent range, or Citigroup, which typically weighs in at about 20 percent.

Nevertheless, Fannie and Freddie saw huge gains in their earnings from 1998 through 2003. Let's consider Fannie, the larger and older of the two. The company earned about $3.4 billion in 1998. By 2001, Fannie's net income rose to $5.9 bil-lion, as the housing market heated up and demand for Fannie's mortgage-backed securities rose.

In July of 2000, Fannie sold for about $50 a share but the company's stock to $86.75 by the end of the year. Its dividend soared from 28 cents a share in 2000 to 52 cents a share in 2004. Although the stock didn't shoot the moon, it was considered a reliable, if unexciting, growth stock.

How did Fannie earn all that money? In a word, volume. In 1998, Fannie had $637 billion of mortgage-backed securities outstanding. By 2002, it had more than $1 trillion; by 2007, the company's mortgage-backed securities topped $2 trillion. In addition, the company retained some mortgages for its own investment portfolio—nearly $724 million by 2007.

Fannie Mae and Freddie Mac did some dabbling in subprime loans, but by and large, its lending standards were strong, and its default rates were low. In 1998, just 0.56 percent of its loans defaulted. Its highest default rate was in 1984, when it hit 1.65 percent.

As the companies grew, however, questions about them began to mount. In 2003, for example, both had to restate their earnings when questions were raised about their accounting policies. (In Freddie Mac's case, the company had understated earnings by $5 billion.) In addition, both companies became Washington powerhouses, spending $3.5 billion on lobbying efforts in the first three months of 2008 and employing some 42 lobbying firms, according to National Public Radio.[1]

But the biggest questions, at least in terms of the companies' futures, came from Wall Street. The basic question: What would happen if defaults on Freddie- and Fannie-backed mortgages started to spike, just as subprime mortgages did?

---

[1]**How Fannie, Freddie Became Kings of the Hill**
by Peter Overby, Morning Edition, July 15, 2008. http://www.npr.org/templates/story/story.php?storyId=92540620

It was a good question. By 2008, Freddie and Fannie owned or guaranteed $5.2 trillion of home mortgages—or about 50 percent of the entire U.S. mortgage market. But they had only $81 billion in capital, only enough to cover 1.6 percent of the mortgages they insure. Should defaults rise above the 1984 worst-case scenario, the companies would be bankrupt.

Given the nerve-racking environment of mid-2008, a spike in mortgage defaults began to seem increasingly likely. Not only were foreclosures mounting, but so were pressures on the U.S. consumer and the economy in general. At $140 a barrel, gasoline had topped $4 a gallon. Much of the government's economic stimulus checks—$600 for single filers, $1,200 for those married and filing jointly—were going to the gas pump, not to the local Ford dealer.

Even worse, big cracks were starting to appear in the banking system. Bank failures, which were extremely low in 2007, began to rise. The most startling was the collapse of IndyMac Bank, one of the nation's top mortgage lenders. Its failure was the third-largest in the history of the Federal Deposit Insurance Corp., and caused minor riots in California a few days after the failure was announced.

The week of July 7, both Fannie and Freddie stock took a pounding. On Friday, July 11, Fannie stock plunged 22 percent, closing at $10.25—an 80 percent loss for the year.

The cavalry, in the form of the Treasury and the Federal Reserve, rode in over the weekend. One of the charms of Freddie Mac and Fannie Mae is that they are government-sponsored enterprises, or GSEs. Because the government started them, investors have long figured that the government will support them if they get into trouble. And, indeed, both Fannie and Freddie had a $2.5 billion line of credit with the Treasury, should things ever get tight.

Late on Sunday, the Treasury sent out a release, which read:

July 13, 2008
HP-1079

Paulson Announces GSE Initiatives

Washington, DC—Treasury Secretary Henry M. Paulson, Jr. issued the following statement:

Fannie Mae and Freddie Mac play a central role in our housing finance system and must continue to do so in their current form as shareholder-owned companies. Their support for the housing market is particularly important as we work through the current housing correction.

GSE debt is held by financial institutions around the world. Its continued strength is important to maintaining confidence and stability in our financial system and our financial markets. Therefore we must take steps to address the current situation as we move to a stronger regulatory structure.

In recent days, I have consulted with the Federal Reserve, OFHEO, the SEC, Congressional leaders of both parties and with the two companies to develop a three-part plan for immediate action. The President has asked me to work with Congress to act on this plan immediately.

First, as a liquidity backstop, the plan includes a temporary increase in the line of credit the GSEs have with Treasury. Treasury would determine the terms and conditions for accessing the line of credit and the amount to be drawn.

Second, to ensure the GSEs have access to sufficient capital to continue to serve their mission, the plan includes temporary authority for Treasury to purchase equity in either of the two GSEs if needed.

Use of either the line of credit or the equity investment would carry terms and conditions necessary to protect the taxpayer.

Third, to protect the financial system from systemic risk going forward, the plan strengthens the GSE regulatory reform legislation currently moving through Congress by giving the Federal Reserve a consultative role in the new GSE regulator's process for setting capital requirements and other prudential standards.

I look forward to working closely with the Congressional leaders to enact this legislation as soon as possible, as one complete package.

In a word: The government will do whatever necessary to keep Fannie and Freddie afloat.

The details of the action—all but the third item will need Congressional approval—are fairly extraordinary. First, the Treasury is saying that it will lend Freddie and Fannie as much money as they should need over the next 18 months or so. The exact amount will be the subject of negotiation between the Treasury and the two companies.

Secondly, the Treasury will actually infuse the companies with capital, if necessary. Basically, this means that the government will take an ownership position in Freddie or Fannie, should the companies need more capital.

If you owned a bond issued by either company, you were a happy, happy person on Monday, July 14. Essentially, the Treasury's announcement meant that your bonds were as creditworthy as the Treasury's. (Most people on Wall Street had figured that out by Friday, when Freddie and Fannie's bond prices began to soar). There was no way you were going to get stiffed on your loans to the two mortgage giants.

Stockholders were reassured, but not quite as much: Fannie and Freddie stock remained in the single digits. The Treasury was generous with bondholders, but stockholders, as they had learned from Bear Stearns, weren't at the back of the line. They weren't in the line at all. And if Fannie and Freddie raised more capital, it mean that the value of their shares would be worth less, all things being equal.

Stockowners got one small bone, however: The Securities and Exchange Commission decided to curb short selling in the companies' stock. Short selling, as you recall, is a way to bet that a stock's price will fall. You borrow shares from your broker, sell them, and, if the stock tumbles, repurchase them later at a lower price. The difference between your selling price and your buying price is your profit.

Fannie and Freddie had become the bear's playground in 2008. Sellers had sold 77 million Freddie shares short, or 12 percent of its stock. Another 140 million shares of Fannie were short. The SEC's move curbed naked short selling, which is nowhere near as racy as you might think. It means that you sell the stock short without borrowing the necessary shares first.

What was particularly unusual was that the SEC extended the 30-day ban on naked shorting to 17 other major financial firms, including Goldman Sachs and Merrill Lynch. In addition, the SEC began doling out subpoenas to hedge funds that had been shorting financials heavily, in a not-too-subtle reminder that there are laws, after all, for spreading false rumors about a company. (Bears are notorious for badmouthing companies that they are short.)

The final piece of the Treasury's announcement was also extraordinary: Fannie and Freddie would be able to borrow at the Fed's discount window, a privilege normally reserved for troubled banks. But the Fed had opened the discount window for Bear Stearns as well. It made its discount window available for Fannie and Freddie because the Treasury's proposal required Congressional approval before it could be implemented. The Fed wanted to reassure investors that no bad things would happen before Congress stepped in.

And, at least on Monday, July 14, the markets held. Freddie Mac was able to sell $3 billion of its own corporate debt that day without Federal assistance. Both companies' stock prices, while down miserably, firmed a bit from their all-time lows.

We must leave our story on a note of high drama. On July 15, president Bush weighed in on the economy and the financial system, doing what presidents do in these situations: Telling everyone that things will be fine. "We're going through a tough time, but our economy has continued growing, consumers are spending, businesses are investing, exports continue increasing, and American productivity remains strong. We can have confidence in the long-term foundation of our economy, and I believe we will come through this challenge stronger than before."

Fed Chairman Ben Bernanke, whose job had become grueling in the past few months, was far less upbeat. "The economy continues to face numerous difficulties," Bernanke told a Senate committee hearing, "including ongoing strains in financial markets, declining house prices, a softening labor market, and rising prices of oil, food, and some other commodities.

Things are always darkest, investment manager Peter Lynch was fond of saying, just before they're pitch black. Whether Fannie or Freddie will remain in the same form, as privately owned yet publicly guaranteed entities, is anyone's guess. Certainly, bank failures will rise in 2008 and, if previous banking crises are any guide, the troubles in the banking system will last well into the next economic recovery. But sooner or later—and we certainly hope sooner—the economy will recover, earnings and personal income will rise, and life will be good again. And—you can count on this—somewhere in the next recovery will be the seeds of the next new financial mania. Don't you fall for it.

Notes

Chapter 1: What Just Happened Here?

1. "JP Morgan Bags Wounded Bear—Bargain-basement $235 million for Reeling Giant," *New York Post,* 17 March 2008, p. 29.

2. Panzer, Michael. "Buffett on Derivatives: 'A Fool's Game.'" Posted May 7, 2007. http://seekingalpha.com/article/34606-buffett-on-derivatives-a-fool-s-game.

Chapter 2: How Did It All Begin?

1. "Measuring Worth." www.measuringworth.com.

2. Waggoner, John & Shell, Adam. "You might recall your parents or grandparents talking about it. Falling prices. Rising unemployment. Global recession. Financial collapse. Depression," *USA Today,* 27 May 2003, p. 1B.

3. Department of the Treasury, Board of Governors of the Federal Reserve System, Federal Housing Finance Board, Moody's Investors Service, and Standard & Poor's. "Bond yields and interest rates, 1929–2007." http://www.gpoaccess.gov/eop/2008/B73.xls.

4. Standard & Poor's Home Price History: January 1987–January 2008. http://www2.standardandpoors.com/spf/pdf/index/CS_HomePrice_History_032544.xls.

5. Grillo, Thomas. "October home sales leap in state to gain 20.8% over last year, but prices moderating," *The Boston Globe*, 26 November 2006, p. D1.

6. Jares, Andrea. "Existing home sales up 9 percent in October," *San Antonio Star-Telegram,* 22 November 2003.

7. Robinson-Jacobs, Karen. "Home sales still hot in Southland; Prices in Los Angeles and Orange Counties also are up sharply over a year ago. Agents expect a strong November." *Los Angeles Times,* 19 November 2003, sect. C, p. 2.

8. "A record-setting year for the housing industry," *Miami Herald,* 28 December 2003, p. H2.

9. Morris, Evan. "The Word Detective." Issue February 16, 2005. http://www.word-detective.com/021605.html.

10. U.S. Census Bureau, Housing and Household Economic Statistics Division. Last revised: December 2, 2004. http://www.censusbureau.biz/hhes/www/housing/census/historic/owner.html.

11. "The Bonus Army" Eye Witness to History, www.eyewitnesstohistory.com (2000).

12. New Deal Network. http://newdeal.feri.org/timeline/1933c2.htm.

13. Digital History: Using New Technologies to Enhance Teaching and Research. "1930s: The First 100 Days." http://www.digitalhistory.uh.edu/database/article_display.cfm?HHID=468.

14. Ashbrook Center for Public Affairs. Campaign Speech: Franklin D. Roosevelt. Franklin D. Roosevelt. October 24, 1932. Atlanta, GA. http://teachingamericanhistory.org/library/index.asp?document=85.

15. *Time Magazine.* "Profitable HOLC." April. 22, 1946. http://www.time.com/time/magazine/article/0,9171,792832,00.html.

16. Fannie Mae Foundation. "Frequently Asked Questions: Current Loan Limits." Last revised: July 7, 2006. http://www.fanniemae.com/faq/faq3.jhtml?p=FAQ

Chapter 3: Silly Season

1. Greenberg, Betty. "Value soars on choice hub parking spots,"*Boston Globe,* 14 April 2004.

2. Satzman, Darrell. "Hotter than Beverly Hills 90210: As some upscale spots cooled, lower-priced communities sizzled in the latter half of 2004: Lynwood 90262 was among places to buy," *Los Angeles Times,* 20 March 2005, sect. K, p. 1.

3. Smith, Hubble. "Talk of a housing bubble isn't confined to Las Vegas Strip," *Chicago Tribune,* 22 October 2003, p. 10.

4. Van Voorhis, Scott. "Local condo flippers may be in too deep," *Boston Herald,* 22 December 2005, p. 42.

5. Hanks, Douglas, III. "Flipping out?" *Miami Herald,* 26 July 2004, sect. G, p. 22.

6. Insana Ron. "Home builder optimistic in his outlook for market." *USA Today,* 3 October 2005, sect. B, p. 4.

7. Kirchhoff, Sue and Krantz, Matt. "How high can they go?" *USA Today,* 27 May 2004, sect. B, p. 1.

8. Kirchhoff, Sue and Krantz, Matt. "How high can they go?" *USA Today,* 27 May 2004, sect. B, p. 1.

9. Shepard, Alicia C. "The Giant Pool of Money." NPR Org. http://www.npr.org/ombudsman/2008/05/the_giant_pool_of_money.html.

10. Henry, David and Goldstein, Matthew. "The Bear Flu: How to Spread. A novel financing scheme used by Bear's hedge funds became a template for subprime disaster," *Business Week,* 31 December 2007, p. 30.

11. Henry, David and Goldstein, Matthew. "The Bear Flu: How to Spread. A novel financing scheme used by Bear's hedge funds became a template for subprime disaster," *Business Week,* 31 December 2007, p. 30.

Chapter 4: Matters Become More Serious

1. "Greenspan Still Sees Froth." Thestreet.com. June 9, 2005. http://www.thestreet.com/markets/marketfeatures/10227286.html

2. "Bernanke: No housing bubble," Home Equity Wire, unbylined, July 15, 2005, pg 1. vol. 3, no. 22.

3. Realtor.Org. Market-by-Market Home Price Analysis Reports. October 2005. http://web.archive.org/web/20051126044138/http://www.realtor.org/research.nsf/pages/anti-bubblereports.

4. Knox, Noelle. "Paying for a roof over your head—but not much else," *USA Today,* 12 September 2007, sect. B, p. 1.

5. Schnurman, Mitchell. "Slump in housing could be ominous," *Ft. Worth Star-Telegram,* 11 February 2007, p. 1.

6. Daniels, Steve and Fields-White, Monee. "Foreclosure fallout: Aftereffects of subprime lending binge cripple communities across Chicago area," *Crain's Chicago Business,* 21 April 2008, news; p. 1.

7. Madigan, Patrick. "Subprime Foreclosures." http://www.iowafinanceauthority.gov/documents/Patrick_Madigan.pdf.

8. Grollmus, Denise. "Meet the biggest predatory lender in Cleveland—America's new ambassador to the Netherlands," *Cleveland Scene,* 19 October 2005.

9. Kelley, Kate. "The fall of Bear Stearns," a three-part series. *The Wall Street Journal,* May 27–May 29, 2008.

Chapter 5: Where Do We Go from Here?

1. Belton, Beth. "Falling oil prices good but also bad," *USA Today,* 30 November 1998, sect. B, p 1.

2. Carroll, Lewis. "Through the Looking-Glass and What Alice Found There." http://etext.lib.virginia.edu/etcbin/toccer-new2?id=CarGlas.sgm&images=images/modeng&data=/texts/english/modeng/parsed&tag=public&part=2&division=div1.

3. Devine, Danny. National Town Hall Forum Preview Are Americans Still Lost in Space About Social Security Reform? June 30, 1998. http://www.ebri.org/publications/prel/index.cfm?fa=prelDisp&content_id=323.

Chapter 7: Fighting Depression

1. Economic Report of the President, 2008, table b79, U.S. Government Printing Office.

2. Department of the Treasury/Federal Reserve Board. "MAJOR FOREIGN HOLDERS OF TREASURY SECURITIES (in billions of dollars). June 16, 2008. http://www.treas.gov/tic/mfh.txt.

3. Wagner, P. and Bartko, John K. Standard and Poor's. Subprime Mortgage Lenders: Transition In A Stressed Mortgage Cycle. May 8, 2007. http://www2.standardandpoors.com/portal/site/sp/en/us/page.article/3,1,1,0,1148444105578.html.

Chapter 8: Creeping Inflation

1. *Federal Reserve Bank of San Francisco.* FRBSF Economic Letter: 2001-20. July 13, 2001. Last Updated December 3, 2007. http://www.frbsf .org/publications/economics/letter/2001/el2001-20.html.

2. CNN.com/world. "Zimbabwe inflation tops 24,000 percent, officially." February 1, 2008. http://www.cnn.com/2008/WORLD/africa/02/01/ zimbabwe.inflation.ap/index.html.

About the Author

John Waggoner is a personal finance reporter for *USA Today*, where he has worked since 1989, covering mutual funds, stocks, bonds, and the economy. Waggoner also writes a weekly column, "Investing," for *USA Today*. The column covers all facets of personal investing, from portfolio theory to picking individual stocks. He's a regular contributor to *The Nightly Business Report* on PBS. Waggoner is the author of *Money Madness: Strange Schemes and Extraordinary Manias on and off Wall Street*, as well as *The Fast Forward MBA in Investing*, both published by Wiley. He's co-author of *The Busy Family's Guide to Money*. Waggoner has a B.A. and M.A. in English from Northeastern University, and began his business writing career at *Donoghue's Money Fund Report*, now *IBC Money Fund Report*. Prior to joining *USA Today*, he was a senior editor at *The Independent Investor*, and he lives in northern Virginia.

Index

Index

Index

Index